The RTE Writer's Guide

Martin Devaney has a degree in drama from Trinity College. He has written for stage, radio and film. His plays have been performed around Ireland, as well as Canada, Australia and Poland. He writes extensively for RTE; broadcasted work includes one-off plays, series, comedies and children's plays. He has written/produced a comedy quiz series for RTE. He has also written for the BBC. Radio Slovakia and Radio Norway are to broadcast a series of his shortly. He lectures extensively on creative writing in Ireland and abroad.

THE RTE WRITER'S GUIDE

A GUIDE FOR THE PROFESSIONAL WRITER AND ANYONE INTERESTED IN BROADCAST WRITING

MARTIN DEVANEY

RTÉ
Published in association with
Radio Teilifís Éireann

BLACKWATER PRESS

808.02/354894

© Martin Devaney, 1995

Produced in Ireland by Blackwater Press

Broomhill Business Park, Tallaght, Dublin

ISBN 0 86121 632 6

Editor: Ríona MacNamara

Dedication

For Nora and Paddy, would that I had their energy ,

and 2C without whom . . .

CONTENTS

PART I THE BUSINESS OF WRITING

PART II RADIO

PART III TELEVISION & FILM

FOREWORD

In this era of dependency on things technological to occupy one's mind, it is a pleasure to preface a book that deals with the 'nuts and bolts' of creative writing. The sections dealing with the world of radio will be of particular interest to aspiring writers.

It is the medium of the future, accessible, portable and boundless for the imaginative. It is an essential guide for writers who have the talent to create 'castles in the air', a 'stampede of elephants from one shrill trumpet and who sees regiments of cavalry in flickering firelight'.

These are the stuff that media dreams are made of, and the 'Bard' will not mind the misquote, as I have done it often in the course of making his words accessible to a far greater audience than he could have dreamt was possible.

This is the magic of broadcasting, and when you absorb Martin Devaney's succinct approach, a new world is awaiting each and everyone who puts pen to paper.

Of course, acceptance is not guaranteed. However, think of every returned script as another valuable lesson rather than a rejection of your efforts.

LAURENCE FOSTER

Editor Radio Drama, RTE

ACKNOWLEDGMENTS

Many people within and without RTE gave generously of their time and their expertise in the compilation of this book. They deserve much of the credit for what is accurate within these pages; any mistakes are my own. The persons I owe a particular debt to include: Claire Keegan (writer), Brian Lally (researcher), Jackie Devaney (secretary), Laurence Foster (Editor, Radio Drama), Aidan C. Mathews (radio drama producer/writer), Ed Brannigan (writer), Daniel Reardon (radio drama producer/writer), John McKenna (producer), Paddy Glackin (Editor, Features & Documentaries), Lorelei Harris (producer), Michael Littleton (Managing Editor Features & Documentaries, RTE Radio), Seamus Hosey (Managing Editor Arts & Drama, RTE Radio), Sean McCarthy (*Glenroe* Script Editor), Claire Duignan (independent television commissioner), Wesley Burrows (scriptwriter), Mary Halpin (former *Fair City* senior Storyline Editor), Pádhraic Ó Ciardha (Editor, Development, Media and Information, Teilifís na Gaeilge), Niall Mathews (Editor Television Entertainment), Vanessa Finlow (Drama Script Editor, Entertainment), Jimmy Murakami (Alegro animation director), Aidan Hickey (Alegro animation director), Alan Gilsenan (documentary-maker), Steve Woods (Anamú founding member), Emmet Harten (animation producer/director), Paul Irvine (producer), John O'Connor (Managing Director, Blackwater Press), Anna O'Donovan (Editorial Manager, Blackwater Press), Ríona MacNamara (editor).

INTRODUCTION

'Writing – the insatiate art of scribbling.'
William Gifford, journalist (1756–1826)

It has happened at some writing workshop or other that I've been asked for any recommended writing textbooks and I've trotted out several of the best.

Predictably, there are questions about writing for Irish radio or television. Some sort of cachet associated with writing for RTE – the sole broadcaster responsible for the Republic – has developed. A story broadcast on RTE marks an important benchmark in the lives of many writers. For some it represents a significant step up on a writing career; for others it is a recognition that their writings have value. For all there is the possibility of that sweet, intense satisfaction achieved from beating off fierce competition.

There was, however, no textbook that I could recommend for intending RTE writers, because none existed. Now, while individual RTE departments do prepare useful leaflets about specific competitions, these are not, nor would they claim to be, comprehensive documents. It became obvious that a publication was necessary that would contain in a single volume all the information which RTE normally provides. This volume would also need to contain answers to the most common writer's questions – what are the do's and don'ts of short-story writing? What do RTE producers like to see arriving on their desks? What do they hate? What actually happens to unsolicited manuscripts? How much can you earn?

The RTE Writer's Guide became an inevitable response to this need, and is intended to assist both the aspiring and professional writer in gaining access to the RTE broadcasting network.

While this book concerns itself with practical ways in which potential RTE writers can directly access the RTE network, it also delves into the back-door route. No book about writing for RTE would be complete without some discussion on independent production companies, as well as incorporating details about accessing script development funds.

You should also be aware that RTE is a flexible organisation which adjusts its programming constantly in response to audience demands, competition or a host of other factors which cannot possibly be anticipated at the time of going to press. No publication can ever therefore be entirely comprehensive – a drama slot that has existed for years might be axed with little warning; a competition date may change following a shake-up of the schedules; a sponsor may unexpectedly decide to promote a product on the back of a short-story competition. Prospective RTE writers are thus advised to remain posted of current developments by purchasing *The RTE Guide* regularly and tuning into the RTE network.

Rather than employing long-winded terminology and constant repetition, a shorthand methodology is used instead. 'Scripts' is generally an abbreviation of 'manuscripts', and the use of 'stories' usually refers to generic comments about television, film and/or radio writing, and not specifically to short stories. 'RTE' itself stands, of course, for Radio Telefís Éireann.

PART I
THE BUSINESS OF WRITING

STARTING OUT

It has to be said that many successful writers are not necessarily good writers, and many good writers are not successful. Skill does not automatically ensure success. Literary history is peppered with the anecdotes of how some writers got their 'big breaks'. Many writers have been 'discovered' after winning a particular writing competition, or they might happen to drop an unsolicited manuscript onto a particular editor's desk, and, joy of joys, their opus is just what the editor is looking for.

Successful writers are often likely to be the ones who possess writing skills and a canny instinct as to what sells, what might be considered for broadcast, and what won't. Successful writers research their markets and target their scripts accordingly. They drop their work off to the very person who requires it, and it is no coincidence that the format and presentation of the work is just what that particular editor likes to see. Close examination reveals that these writers often manufacture their own luck; such a writer, aware of an annual competition and gambling that it will be held again, starts writing well in advance of the official announcements; such a writer, while attending a talk given by a publisher, carefully notes a stray comment about future publishing trends and, the very next morning, places a strong mug of coffee on the desk before lifting off the typewriter's dust cover.

These writers realise that in this technological age, people who wouldn't have the patience to use an old Remington easily spew out reams of good-looking computer-generated script. Aspiring writers face fierce competition as they strive to ensure that their script doesn't become lost in a broadcaster's unsolicited-manuscript mountain. Writers initially do have the odds stacked against them. Successful writers, leaving little to chance, see what they can do to improve those odds.

PRESENTATION

This book concerns itself with increasing the odds of getting your work broadcast on the RTE network. While presentation is not the most important of the topics discussed, its impact should not be dismissed. A poorly presented script will only lessen the impact of your story. RTE does not expect publication-standard scripts, and it does make allowances for new writers who are perfectly entitled, if not counted on, to make mistakes. Even professional writers sometimes get confused over 'crossfades' and 'cut tos'.

Work that has merit will almost always be developed. Your job as a writer is to get your script to the stage where it is accepted for broadcast or development. This stage is not easily reached if your script gives a reader a migraine. It is important to realise that the readers of your submissions are human too; they have failings just like anyone else and it is important to get them on your side – a good story badly presented may eventually get broadcast, but it stands a greater chance of rejection than a well-presented submission. You want to captivate the script readers so that after reading one page they are so eager to see what happens next that they forget the passing of time, they forget the mortgage repayments, they forget to pick the kids up from school.

Common submission errors can turn a reader's pleasurable experience into a struggle – a bad photocopy of a bad photocopy of a script is as hard for a reader to read as it is for anyone. Maybe the characters aren't indicated properly – maybe the reader has constantly to flick back to the script's beginning to check on who, exactly, is this 'Mrs P'. Your story may ultimately be short listed but you have made this prospect more difficult by submitting a manuscript with built-in distractions. There are several key factors you should take into account before dropping your script in the post.

- Use an appropriately sized envelope for your submission. A script shoe-horned into an envelope tends to burst free moments before arrival.

- Submissions should contain a *brief* covering letter similar to the specimens included in this publication. Ensure the submission is properly addressed.

- Pages should be the standard A4 size (210 mm by 297 mm), typed on one side of the page only, leaving a generous margin all round.

- The paper you use should be clean, white and not so cheap as to be transparent.

- Always remember to place your name and address prominently on the manuscript.

- Where relevant, always include character listings, script synopsis, treatment, et cetera.

- Generally, lines should be double spaced, as this paragraph is. There is enough of a gap between these lines for another complete line if necessary. This blank space is useful for readers'/producers' pencilled-in comments. You may also use it to correct the odd word here or there that you missed in the drafting stage.

- Ensure that all the pages are numbered sequentially.

- The submitted script should be securely though not permanently bound. A staple on the top left-hand corner is preferable to a spiral-bound submission, as the former, with the staple removed, is easier to photocopy. This could be complemented by a cheap slide-on plastic spine with perhaps a clear plastic cover to protect the outer pages.

- Each medium has a different script format, and it is worthwhile studying them and presenting your script in the appropriate layout. You really are wasting your time sending in a stage play to Radio Arts & Drama and asking them if they think it would make a good radio play. First, no one will thank you for not taking the time to adapt it; and second, a potential adaptation is only as good as the writer who adapts it. Have you ever seen a film and bemoaned the fact that it wasn't as good as the book? No reader will be enthused by someone who hasn't made a real effort. You'll find specific guidelines regarding layouts later in this book.

- Technical directions. Don't worry untowardly if you are confused about a script's technical directions. If you are writing a film script you may not know, for example, whether it is best to write CROSSFADE or CUT TO between certain scenes. Script editors do appreciate efforts to get the layouts right – it shows you have an awareness of the medium as well as demonstrating that you are a writer who does your homework – but they don't expect textbook submissions. It is more important to be as accurate as you can. Make your best guess; you will make mistakes, but RTE allows for that.

- Do not submit handwritten material. Type all manuscripts. RTE does not expect writers to provide everything in a neat laser-print format; what they do expect, however, if the script is from a manual typewriter, is that the ribbon is new. Although there is an increase in the number of computer-generated manuscripts sent to RTE, this does not mean that you should feel obliged to compete by spending a small fortune on a word processor. A good story tapped out on a portable typewriter will take precedence over a dull story that had been laser-printed. Radio drama producer Aidan C. Mathews says:

> I think there is an inverse ratio of talent between the persons who use computers and the scripts that they furnish. Very often the impeccably produced computer script is rather desolate while very frequently a script hammered out on a portable QWERTY from the 1950s has everything that it takes to bring us pleasure.

- Finally, remember to keep a copy of your manuscript. RTE doesn't often lose scripts – but it has happened.

UNSOLICITED MANUSCRIPTS

At present, when a writer sends in an unsolicited manuscript to RTE, they normally receive within a week a postcard or letter acknowledging that their script has arrived safely. What happens to the script next depends on where it is sent. The procedure for the processing of a script in the radio centre varies slightly from that of the television centre.

RADIO CENTRE

The first thing that happens to an unsolicited play manuscript is that the name of the play, its writer and the arrival date are entered into a large volume, and an acknowledgement sent.

The script is passed on to the script editor – a professional reader who works outside RTE. The script editor makes an assessment of the manuscript before sending it back into Arts & Drama, where it is read by at least two producers. Then the script, with all the readers' comments, is forwarded to the Editor, Radio Drama, who decides if it should be passed on to producers for development or broadcast, or rejected outright. This whole process takes time, and on average, writers should expect to receive a formal decision between two and three months from the time of submission. If this time has passed without any word, then you may write off a brief note with your query, mentioning your name, the exact title and the date the script was acknowledged.

The procedure for a radio short story is virtually identical to above. See The Francis MacManus Awards, page 22.

TELEVISION CENTRE

The procedure for television scripts is similar to the above, except that the script editor works in-house and tends to short-circuit the system by filtering out unsuitable material. If the submission has potential and is intended to be included in an existing programme or series (perhaps it's a short sketch or a sample episode) it may be passed on to the production assistant of the relevant programme, who in turn passes it on to the programme's producer. If the submission is something like a drama or a comedy with no clear slot, it is assessed and, if it has potential, sent to the editor of the relevant section.

Script editors make themselves aware of just what the producers or the senior editors are looking for. If your script, in their judgement, does not reach a certain standard, it simply won't be seen by the senior editor with the power to commission the work. Even if addressed to the senior editor it will be passed on (usually unread unless you're a well-known writer or known to the editor) to someone else for assessment.

MAKING THE BROADCASTER'S SHORT LIST

While there is no formal classification, submissions for television and radio could be said, to all intents and purposes, to fall into three categories.

The C-pile is for submissions which are more or less immediately returned to the writer with a standardised card saying that there is no room in the schedules for this manuscript. There are several reasons why submissions fall into this category.

- The work may be far too short or long for the available slots.

- The writers might display a patent lack of knowledge of the particular medium they're trying to write for.

- The submission might be a poor version of an existing programme.

- The submission might be far too expensive to be made into a programme. It is easy to write 'And then the bridge over the Rhine explodes'. It's not cheap to make.

- The submission might be too explicit or contain themes which have already been broadcast.

- The submission may be libellous.

- The submission might be illegible.

- The submission may be in the wrong format. A radio script sent into the TV Centre accompanied by a brief cover note enquiring if the play might make good TV is unacceptable.

With the best will in the world, RTE cannot comprehensively detail why submissions are rejected. There are far too many scripts submitted for this to be possible. The Radio Centre receives an average of two scripts a day, seven days a week, every week – which adds up. A producer may write a few lines suggesting ways the script might be improved, but this should not be taken as some sort of implicit guarantee that, should the changes be made, the script will be then accepted. RTE will try to be encouraging but is under no obligation to take any script – even if it's good.

The B-pile is reserved for manuscripts which do contain a certain potential. The writer seems to display a knowledge of the medium and knows what slot he or she wants. The script may, however, have some flaw which mitigates against it. Perhaps the play is the wrong running length; perhaps the ending is unsatisfactory. These scripts are returned with a brief, personalised note indicating where, in the reader's mind, the script is going awry. The writer should then carefully think through the suggestions, and if they feel that they are helpful, should rewrite the script. This rewritten script will have a better chance of being accepted.

The A-pile is for work which is more or less finished. These are submissions which have a good running time, are written for the appropriate medium, and whose writer demonstrates that he or she possesses creative flair and can tell a story well. A-pile writers are aware of the advantages and limitations of the particular medium they are writing for. There is also a likely slot for the work. Submissions in this category have a good chance of being broadcast. Unfortunately for the writer, even an A-category manuscript isn't automatically included in the production schedules. It is possible that a story with a virtually identical theme has just been broadcast – it happens; on the other hand, maybe your story is just what the editor is looking for.

SUBMISSION TIPS

You will enhance your chances of your script being considered if you ask yourself a number of questions before forwarding it to RTE.

- Is it the right length? If it's a story, does it have the required number of words?

- Are you happy that the dialogue sounds plausible?

- Are the characters interesting? Are they clichéd or stereotyped?

- Are there too many characters? Are there many characters of the same sex, with similar ages and accents? Does this lead to confusion?

- Is the manuscript overwritten? If so, where?

- Is the ending appropriate, melodramatic, implausible?

- Is the submission a thinly disguised variation of an existing story?

- If it's a screenplay, will the film be too costly to make? Are all the crowd scenes necessary? Are the special effects vital? Can a number of scenes take place on the same set?

- Is the story well told? How could it be improved?

- Do you have any particular audience/slot in mind for your submission?

You should sit back and objectively analyse your script, noting its good and bad points. Don't treat the script-reader as a proof-reader. Don't send off the script until you are as happy as you're likely to be with it, bearing in mind that you probably will never be entirely satisfied. It might be helpful to know that most professional writers, on hearing their work broadcast, feel uneasy about certain lines or passages.

Several months down the line, a producer may send you a note saying that the play has merits but that certain areas need improving. If this flaw is something that, deep down, you were already aware of, why didn't you remedy it before you submitted the script? Don't expect your reader to be generous.

A common problem, particularly in regard to competitions, is that you may rush off your script because of a rapidly approaching deadline. 'If I'd just one more day, it would have been better' is a frequent lament. Of course the best and obvious approach is to start the play earlier. The closing date for the P.J. O'Connor Awards is normally in late September – if you know you want to enter it, why not start now? Finish the play in plenty of time, finish two plays. If the closing date is only days away, start preparing for next year's competition. Many writers gain tremendous satisfaction from sending off entries for competitions several weeks early; as the closing date approaches, they can then relax and concentrate on something else.

It is often a good idea to place your play or story in a drawer for a month or so before digging it out again for one last look. Your memory of your writing will have faded somewhat. In many respects it will be like reading a stranger's story with only a vague awareness of how it turns out. This approach can have startling results – a story which you felt at the time of writing to be a witty comedy may now seem only mildly amusing. Flaws you were unaware of will leap out at you; you realise that your tenth-century heroine could not have slid down the castle drainpipe because (a) it would have been impossible wearing that voluminous ball-gown you spent two pages describing; and (b) castles didn't have drainpipes . . . .

You could also benefit from getting a third opinion. However, beware of the advice of those nearest and dearest to you – they may tell you what you want to hear rather than what you need to be told. Good writers' groups may prove to be a more productive option. They may spot areas where the story can be improved. A danger is that participants will give lots of well-meaning advice and be disappointed if you don't use it; however, they are not automatically right. It would be a mistake to incorporate every suggestion into your work. Writers who are too polite produce safe, dull writing.

Writing courses, often given by established writers, also have their uses and are a good source of writing advice and tips. They can also be inspiring; when you see how ordinary most writers are, you start to think that perhaps you can write that movie after all.

So now you are as happy as you can be with your work. You've remedied any glaring errors and you've tidied up the dialogue. The script is properly typed and laid out like the specimens in this book. You've made copies. Give yourself a well-deserved pat on the back. You have done what many others have failed to do – you have started *and* finished a story. Now, all you have to do is stick it in an envelope and send it on its way. You can of course personally drop it into the front desk of the Radio or Television Centre if you happen to be passing, but don't try to wrangle a meeting with any of the producers or editors to 'sell' the submission. You can't short-circuit the system, and you would be doing yourself a disservice in attempting to do so.

T H E   C O N T R A C T

If your submitted script is accepted for broadcast, RTE will send you an initial letter indicating acceptance. The contract will follow. Your script will not be produced until you have signed and returned your contract. The contract will usually indicate the name of the work to be broadcast, the rate of payment and the broadcast date, if known. Details of repeat fees are also included. Fees for repeats are normally half of the corresponding rate at the time of broadcast.

You must sign the contract granting RTE permission to broadcast the work, and confirming that you are its true author. A contract may become void if you infringe any copyright or include defamatory material in your work.

You will be paid on return of your signed contract. You do not normally have to wait until your work is broadcast. In fact, your fee will be well spent by the time your script is aired.

THE   PRODUCTION

Once a script is accepted, it is assigned a producer who places it into his or her production schedule. Normally the work is recorded several months before it is broadcast. The broadcast date depends upon the available slots and the nature of the work itself.

RADIO

The radio producer who is also the director of the play is responsible for the entire production, and must deal with everything from sending you your contract to casting the actors. The producer usually has a list of actors – who can play a range of ages and character parts – to choose from. Sorry, but producers are obliged to select only actors with Actors' Equity cards, so even if the play is about your great-aunt's exploits, she can't be in it – unless of course she's in the union.

The producer may consult you with a query about something in the script; perhaps there is a major change that the producer feels is necessary and, if time permits, will want to discuss with you. The editing-out of text to enable a too-long play to fit a particular slot is never done in consultation with the writer.

Sometimes, by the time you receive your contract, the work might even be 'in the can', awaiting transmission. You may be disappointed at what you perceive is a missed opportunity to hear your play being recorded – you are not alone. RTE do not encourage writers to attend recordings. You have provided the play and now you are, in effect, redundant. Once that script is put in the post, it becomes the responsibility of someone else. Many writers find the lack of consultation unsettling. You may have spent many hours working on your play, have given up your social life to nurse your baby and may consequently become excessively proprietorial over your work. This, compounded with a natural reluctance to give up your pride and joy to strangers, means that many writers, given the opportunity of attending a recording, find great difficulty in restraining their comments. Writers have, in the past, insisted on changing text in the studio, pressed the actors to use a particular accent, or harried the producer to redo a scene which wasn't to their satisfaction. This has led to a general reluctance to encourage writers to attend recordings.

> We like authors every now and again to come in for rehearsals. We don't like them at recording – it's not fair, you wouldn't have them on stage the first night. And that's not dismissing them either, it's just they do get in the way – there's no doubt that there is skin and hair flying in our world – lumps under the carpet. But they do benefit from a visit in here, it opens their eyes and it is very necessary. It was a mystery world. Years ago, we were asking people to write for radio and they never even saw a studio, so we encourage them to come in when they send in the script and we say: 'You've got some good ideas for the production, however as writer, your job is done. How about, though, you sit in next week for half an hour and see what the real world is like?'

> *Laurence Foster, Editor Radio Drama*

For what it's worth, you might be curious to know what happens to your script on the recording date. That morning the cast and crew assemble in the studio. The actors, and perhaps a spot-effects person who manages the 'live' sound effects such as a door opening, take their places 'on the floor'.

The producer and a sound engineer, who plays the pre-recorded effects (usually compact discs from the effects library) and who also records the play onto quarter-inch tape – sit in a glass booth overlooking the actors. There may also be a sound supervisor who oversees the recording levels and supervises the special effects.

The play is usually recorded two to three months before transmission. This date is often determined by the nature of the play. If a radio play with a Christmas theme is accepted in January, it may not be recorded until the following November. On the other hand, some radio plays of a topical nature have been accepted and broadcast within a month, though admittedly this is rare.

TELEVISION

Television writing is much the same, except it is fair to say that almost everything takes longer on television. TV dramas are recorded many months (in some cases well over a year) before they are broadcast. 'Live' programmes are the exception. Sketches for programmes such as *The End* are sometimes prepared a week or so before transmission.

A crucial difference between TV and radio is that on TV, a script editor instead of a producer prepares the script for broadcast. If it is a TV drama, the script editor will probably consult you about changing particular scenes, but if the script just needs editing, will probably do it for you. The producer and director also have an input into your script; they may trim back your scenes and even broadcast them in a different order to the way they were written.

P A Y M E N T S

Writers are generally paid by the minute. The amount they are paid depends on their rate, and their rate depends on the amount of material they have had broadcast combined with their professional writing standing.

At present, there are three rates of pay for radio.

- Grade 1. This is for writers who have not more than two hours of work broadcast. The rate of pay is £8.50 per minute. A 28-minute play thus earns the writer £238.

- Grade 2. This is for writers who have had more than two hours but less than six hours of written work broadcast. The rate is £10.30 per minute;

- Grade 3. This is for writers who have had more than six hours' worth of drama broadcast. Their rate is £13.70 per minute.

Adaptations of work from another format have a lesser payment rate.

- Grade 1. £5.56 per minute.

- Grade 2. £6.64 per minute.

- Grade 3. £9.11 per minute.

Writers for *Sunday Miscellany* can expect a £48 one-off payment per broadcast piece regardless of length, and the same fee for two poems.

A radio short story can earn a writer a standard £90 fee.

First-placed competition winners can earn substantially more than these figures. A P.J. O'Connor Award-winning playwright can earn £1,500 for a 30-minute play. A Francis MacManus short story prize-winner can earn the same amount for a fifteen-minute short story.

Television writing is financially more rewarding than radio writing. Payment rates are determined by a number of complex factors, including the nature of the programme and the experience of the writer.

Series are usually written by teams of writers and as a consequence, fees tend to be lower than for original work. Similarly, programmes for peak-time viewing can often attract a higher rate than off-peak programmes.

Most television writers usually have a considerable background in other writing areas such as stage, radio or literature, which means in turn that they already possess some kind of professional standing. This of course affects their payment rates. The exact amount you can expect is therefore difficult to quantify and will probably be subject to negotiation.

The following figures are guidelines only.

- Writers of an original dramatic television play can normally expect a minimum of £3,000 in respect of a one-hour work, and pro-rata for pieces of longer or shorter duration.

- Writers of series or serials may expect about £925 per half-hour.

- Writers of series or serials which are wholly original and written by the individual writer can expect in the region of £1,170 per half-hour.

PART II
RADIO

ARTS & DRAMA

*Writing Slots. Writing Radio Drama. Beginning the
Play. Submission Layouts. Writing Radio Short Stories.*

The Arts & Drama section of RTE Radio was formed after a recent restructuring within the Radio Centre and, as its name suggests, is responsible for all arts and drama programming. Some of the programmes which fall within its jurisdiction include *The Arts Show* and *Sunday Miscellany*. Its overall brief encompasses stories, poetry, plays and any other drama-related programming.

Arts & Drama represents a huge potential market for the radio writer, as it consumes a tremendous amount of material every year. It broadcasts almost 250 hours of dramatic work annually. The output consists of comic plays, serious plays, one-off series, novel adaptations, play-competition winners plus an in-house serial. Every week *Sunday Miscellany* broadcasts short scripts by writers, while the popular Francis MacManus short-story competition takes place every year.

While only established writers are commissioned to write the in-house serial, there are still plenty of other opportunities for the budding writer. RTE has such a voracious appetite for material that it needs a constant supply of plays and stories and consequently writers to write them. Without fresh submissions, the drama slots would dry up and the competitions would cease. Laurence Foster, Editor Radio Drama has always stressed the importance of encouraging new voices:

We had eighteen new writers last year and we had 44 plays by women writers over the last five years. A journalist wrote in the *Irish Times* that only five women had any plays performed by any theatre in the past five years in Dublin – we've had 44. So obviously scripts are being developed. Three women have won the P.J. O'Connor Awards or an award in the P.J. O'Connor Awards in the last three years. We're not doing the plays because 'Oh it's time a woman went on air' – it's because they're writing good stuff. If it's good and we think it's worth developing, we'll do it.

If you have a good idea and take the time to craft it into a finished radio play, then you are already halfway to being considered for broadcast. If this play is written with a particular slot in mind and is the appropriate length, it will have dramatically increased its chances of making it into the RTE schedules. A drama producer can pick up two play scripts, discard one but decide that the other may merit a second reading. There is no real reason why your play – if you have done your homework and have made a carefully thought-out submission – should not fall into the latter category.

Plays should be submitted to: The Editor, Arts & Drama, Radio Centre, RTE, Donnybrook, Dublin 4.

WRITING SLOTS

At present there are several categories of slots which the writer should bear in mind. Writers should be wary – these slots may vary from month to month. In fact, by the time you read this, the slots *will* be different and therefore *The RTE Guide* should be periodically consulted. For what it's worth, at the time of going to press there is a one-hour slot on a Tuesday evening, a half-hour slot on Thursday evening, a fifteen-minute *Booktime* slot weeknights, and the daily soap *RiverRun* which goes out weekdays, twice daily – once at lunchtime and again at dinnertime. There is some flexibility in the schedules and there are occasional six to eight half-hour series plus several 90-minute dramas. A series called *Plays Peculiar* is usually featured in the autumn or spring season. There is also a competition slot geared towards new writers called the P.J. O'Connor Awards, which is broadcast in the spring. Arts & Drama also has plans for a new regular series which will comprise of plays by new writers.

ADAPTATIONS

Arts & Drama is responsible for broadcasts of adaptations of material derived from another medium, such as the stage or novels. The adaptations could be in the form of a one-off 90-minute play or a series.

If you wish to adapt material which isn't your own, there are a couple of points you should be aware of.

- The first is copyright. You may not be allowed to adapt the work. If in doubt, write to the publishers of the work to be adapted or to whoever owns the rights to the work. Generally all literary work becomes out of copyright when the writer has been dead for fifty years.

- The original material could already have been adapted. Most well-known literary works have been broadcast on radio. When in doubt, write to Arts & Drama with a query.

- The original material might already be in the process of being adapted. A book might be just published which you feel would be ideal for adaptation. However, RTE staff read books too and could come up with similar thoughts; in fact, they might get the books before you do, as publishers will often send advance copies to them.

BOOKTIME

This a slot which goes out weeknights. The books are usually classics or pertinent to some contemporary event or activity. A book may have just won some literary prize, or it could be seasonal. Perhaps the author has just died. A book will be read in its entirety, or in a condensed version. Generally it will be the producer who decides how the book should be adapted.

THE FRANCIS MACMANUS AWARDS

The Francis MacManus Awards is a short-story competition for radio and is named after the late short-story writer, novelist and broadcaster who was born in Kilkenny in 1909 and who was General Features Officer in Radio for eighteen years. His novels include *Stand and Give Challenge, Candle for the Proud, Men Withering, The Wild Garden, Flow On Lonely River, Watergate, The Greatest of These* and *The Fire in the Dust*.

This annual competition attracts around a thousand entries every year. The winning entry receives £1,500 and a commemorative award; the three runners-up receive £750, £500 and £250 respectively. Each winning story is broadcast on Radio One. Repeat broadcasts of the story (if any) receive payments at current rates.

Other stories of a high standard may be selected from the entries and are paid at the normal rate.

Prize-winning Radio Stories, a collection of the competition's best stories published by Mercier Press, is available in bookshops and could be a worthy investment for prospective short-story competition entrants.

Entries are usually accepted from June until the closing date, which is normally in late September/early November. Each story is read by a minimum of two readers. There is no entry fee and writers may send in as many works as they wish. The winning entry in 1994 (the ninth year of the competition) was Des Redmond's 'Down at Ray's', a story set in a chip shop. The runners-up were John F. Deane, founder of *Poetry Ireland*, writer Ivy Bannister and writer/journalist Terry Prone.

The usual rules of entry and conditions are as follows.

* The competition is open to anyone born or normally resident in Ireland.

* Stories must be original and not have been previously published in any medium.

* Stories must be written especially for radio.

* Stories may be in English or Irish.

* Entries must be typed and contain between 1,850 and 1,950 words.

* The author's name and address should be clearly written on each story entered for the competition.

* Entries are acknowledged only if accompanied by a SAE.

* Writers are of course advised to retain a copy of the story as manuscripts will not be returned.

Entries should be sent to: The Francis MacManus Awards, RTE Radio 1, Donnybrook, Dublin 4.

NEW WRITERS' SEASON

This is a proposed new series comprising perhaps six plays, all of which will be written by new writers. The scripts will be gleaned from a combination of the unsolicited material sent into RTE and entries to the P.J. O'Connor Awards. It is likely that the plays will be of a standard 30 minutes' duration.

THE P.J. O'CONNOR AWARDS

The late P.J. O'Connor was the head of RTE radio drama and a much-respected radio drama producer, who produced a tremendous number of plays for both the stage and radio, including *Tarry Flynn* and the notorious *The Tailor and Ansty*. He was also a popular adjudicator on the amateur drama circuit.

The initial idea behind these awards was to somehow commemorate both of his passions – radio drama and amateur drama. A balance had to be found between the desires of amateur companies seeking a platform on the national airwaves and the wishes of playwrights, who usually prefer professional actors performing their work. The end result was a competition whereby three plays are selected for professional production by Arts & Drama, and six plays are performed by amateur drama companies under the supervision of RTE producers.

This competition is restricted to new writers or to writers who have had less than two hours of radio drama professionally broadcast. This is an ideal opportunity for the aspiring radio writer, for many potential competitors – established writers – are excluded from entering.

The winning writers can gain prizes of £1,000, £750 and £500 respectively which are, at present, sponsored by Guardian Insurance. Other placed plays gain their writers £250.

Several other plays from the entries are selected for inclusion in the regular RTE schedules. This means that out of the average 250 entries, about ten or fifteen plays will ultimately be broadcast.

The writers of the best sixteen or so plays are invited to participate in a weekend of RTE radio writing workshops which are given by professional writers such as Bernard Farrell, Jim Douglas, Daniel Reardon and RTE producers including the head of radio drama. This means that an entrant who has sent in a play of the correct length that has been specially written for the radio medium has an excellent chance of being considered for broadcast or at least making it to the workshops.

The following rules and conditions apply.

- The play has to be the original work of the writer.

- The writer has to be an Irish resident or citizen.

- The running time of the plays should be 28 minutes.

- The play should be especially written for radio. No stage play will be considered.

- The play may be in Irish or English.

- No entry will be considered after the closing date, which is normally in November. This of course should be confirmed with RTE.

An official entry form is needed and can be picked up by sending an SAE to: The P.J. O'Connor Awards, Arts & Drama, RTE, Donnybrook, Dublin 4. The entry form is accompanied by a brief information pack containing some hints about radio writing, as well as a sample page of radio script.

PLAYS PECULIAR

This is a season of six or eight plays which is usually included in the autumn schedules, and, as its title suggests, is difficult to categorise. These plays normally last 28 minutes, although there are exceptions. Two short plays which together add up to about 28 minutes and which have similar or contrasting themes might be broadcast as a double bill. Plays might often challenge the usual rules for radio drama and may be experimental. This slot might be appropriate for writers who have an unusual vision of the world.

RIVERRUN

This is a new in-house serial created by Daniel Reardon, a former actor on the *Harbour Hotel* serial – he played Willie Bracken for fifteen years. The soap revolves around the characters who live and work in and around the fictitious village of Drumselby. It is broadcast twice daily, five days a week, on Radio One. Each episode lasts about ten minutes and has a listenership of about 300,000. The series runs all year round.

RiverRun began life as a tentative submission which contained sixteen characters – this was later streamlined down to ten due to budgetary restrictions. The characters' biographies each came to about half a page and, apart from detailing their names, ages and occupations, mentioned the purpose each character would serve, who would provide the source of sexual tension, the source of gossip, of scandal, et cetera. Daniel Reardon says that the characters were specially written so that they would be:

> capable of handling any kind of heavy plot; there's a barrister, a psychiatrist, there's a publican, a priest, and a vicar included in the casting. They would certainly be capable of handling heavy plotlines such as unwanted pregnancies, possible abortions, and so on.

At present there are four writers on the show, including Daniel Reardon. Patrick Dawson has had many plays staged and broadcast; Brian Gallagher has written a novel, *The Invincibles*, as well as several stage and radio plays. The newest writer to the series is Derek Chapman, who is an established actor and writer. These writers have strict deadlines to enable the producers to edit scripts and allow the actors time to rehearse. Each writer is allocated eight-week segments which they take responsibility for writing. During this time, they have to be available for last-minute alterations to the plot; if an actor is suddenly unavailable, the script will have to be hastily rewritten.

Daniel Reardon, Laurence Foster, Michael Campion or Aidan C. Mathews normally produce the programme. It is the producers' role to develop the programme's plot with the writers. The direction each story takes is mapped out many months in advance. Producers, for their own peace of mind, prefer writers who can come up with the goods on time, every time. Inexperienced writers are therefore unlikely to be afforded the opportunity to write for the serial. Vacancies will not be advertised. RTE producers would be inclined to contact suitable writers instead.

SERIES

If your opus is too long for the slots already listed, there is always the possibility of having a series broadcast. A series normally consists of six episodes, each 28 minutes in length. There is no specific date for such series which can be pencilled into the schedules at any time.

The guidelines for writing a series are similar to those for a play except that there are some additional pointers which you should be aware of.

- The average series tells the story of a single character or specific set of main characters who appear in most, if not all, of the episodes. This is a convention which listeners have come to expect. Anyone who tunes into, for example, Episode 3 of the BBC radio comedy series *The Hitchhikers' Guide to the Galaxy* would expect to hear the humorous talking book which featured in the previous episodes. Imagine the disappointment of tuning into an episode of *Fawlty Towers* and discovering that Basil didn't appear. There may, of course, be other incidental characters who feature only in a single episode.

- Allowances should be made for listeners who might miss a previous episode. Continuity might recap on previous episodes or they may not – it is prudent to include in each episode some references to the main plot.

- Each episode should be able to tell a story which has a beginning, middle and end. If your series is about two tramps on the road, then perhaps one episode will show them having an altercation with a respectable member of the community. It shouldn't be vital that a listener tune in to the whole series in order to get a sense of who the characters are; otherwise, if they miss an episode, they may feel that there is little point in tuning into any of the broadcasts.

- Each episode of the series should advance a main plot. Perhaps our two tramps are making a journey to a crossroads where they expect someone to appear? Each weekly episode fuels the anticipation of this climactic moment.

SUNDAY MISCELLANY

Sunday Miscellany is broadcast on Sundays from 9.05 a.m. until 9.50 a.m. The programme comprises short scripts, between three and five minutes long, read by the writers themselves and linked by classical music. Scripts can be on any topic of general interest (e.g. history, travel, biography, personal reminiscences). They may also be short literary pieces or poetry.

The producer is keen to emphasise that she is looking for 'high-quality writing'. Many writers, and indeed writers' groups, view the programme as a stepping-stone in their writing careers, believing that a short piece of work is significantly easier to write than a play or short story. The reality, is of course very different. A good *Sunday Miscellany* writer is one who can write a high-quality, entertaining piece concisely. You should also be aware of the sheer bulk of entries submitted to the programme. A writer who may take months to write a play can easily churn out four or five short pieces, and often more, in the same period. This ensures that the producer is inundated with far more material than she can possible use, much of it, it must be said, unusable.

The writer who wishes to be seriously considered for broadcast should take some elementary precautions before submitting.

- The submission should be the correct length – no longer than 700 words or five minutes. It is pointless to submit longer material.

- The submission should be typed. As stated earlier in Presentation, producers do not expect laser-printed masterpieces, but they do expect legible, easy-to-read manuscripts.

- Do not send cassette versions of your submission.

- Covering letters should be short and to the point.

- Submissions should be kept to a minimum. Send only one, perhaps two, of your best pieces. Remember, someone who has already read 30 to 40 unsuitable manuscripts that morning will find it disheartening to open your envelope and have a dozen submissions tumble out. You should know which is your best work; weaker pieces will only lessen its impact. For this reason it is inadvisable for writers' groups to club together and send off their *oeuvres* in the same padded envelope. If your writing is any good, don't dilute it by including it with a pile of unsuitable pieces.

- Submissions should be written for the spoken voice. (See Writing Radio Short Stories, page 72.) Remember that you will be expected to read out your own work, should it be accepted. If you are unable or incapable of adequately conveying your own text, there is no point in submitting. Submittees are paid only if their recording is satisfactory.

Writers may expect a fee of £48 per script or per two poems accepted.

Suitable material should be sent with a self-addressed stamped envelope to: Lorelei Harris, Producer, *Sunday Miscellany*, Radio Centre, RTE, Donnybrook, Dublin 4.

TUESDAY PLAY

This slot lasts for 58 minutes. Plays can be and are about anything. The running length tends to suit dramas and plays about serious issues. This is sometimes the slot for the 'commissioned play', to which established writers are invited to contribute. The running time ensures that most plays are written by writers with considerable experience. It would be rare for an unsolicited manuscript by an inexperienced writer to be up to the standard required.

THURSDAY PLAY

This is a proposed new slot for plays of 28 minutes. Plays can be on any topic and the emphasis will seem to be on entertainment. This is an ideal slot for the writing newcomer or the comedy writer. A 28-minute play is in many respects harder to write than a 60-minute play. Characters have to be introduced and established, and a story begun and completed in half the time. Many writers find that once they have mastered the half-hour form that longer pieces prove to be child's play.

WRITING RADIO DRAMA

For a playwright there can be few media more exacting and challenging than radio. A radio-playwright does not have the luxury of a captive audience who sits in a theatre or cinema prepared to wait until the story gets going or at least until they have got their money's worth. A radio play's audience are a fickle lot who may not even have deliberately set out to listen to your play – they may have tuned in accidentally, and as easily as they happen on to your play, they can swivel that dial away.

It is the radio-playwright's task to make the story as riveting as possible and to create characters as interesting as possible, as quickly as possible, so that the collective fingers of this non-paying audience hesitate over their dials.

The attraction of radio for many playwrights is that plays do not become encumbered with elaborate sets, moody lighting, marvellous costumes or gesticulating actors. Not much comes between the playwright's text and the audience apart from some sound effects and the actors' voices. If the broadcast play is good, you can give yourself a well-deserved pat on the back; however, if the play is bad, there is little the actors or director can do to save it, and there is no one you can blame. The play is the ultimate thing.

Without wishing to be facetious, the first thing the budding radio playwright should be aware of is that radio is for the ear. Your writing should create crisp, clear images which, once heard, are readily visualised. Dialogue must be well paced and flow naturally; scenes should be of varying lengths to avoid monotonous predictability; characters should be appealing – they should be people the listener would like to meet; the story should be teased out to maintain interest but not be so convoluted as to cause confusion.

An advantage of radio over most other media is that effects are cheap. A stage-playwright must write characters who report battles; the radio-playwright can write characters who are right in the thick of them.

The radio play is, however, an unwieldy medium for telling, for instance, the story of a whole football team. It is best to pick one or two of the players and tell the team's story from their points of view.

Every writer is aware that each writing medium has its own specific advantages and limitations. Radio is no exception. A radio-playwright who knows his or her craft tells a story utilising the many advantages of the medium while avoiding the pitfalls.

CHARACTERS

A radio-playwright should create characters so interesting that an audience cares what happens to them. Main characters should be three-dimensional and have characteristics an audience can empathise with and recognise. A story about an accountant at work might be insufferably tedious. However, even accountants have fears, loves, weaknesses – universal qualities we can all understand, and which in turn can draw us into the story. You may dislike accountancy, but you should be attracted to the accountant.

Characters should normally sound as different as possible so that listeners will always be sure who is speaking. Characters of the same age, background and sex will inevitably sound similar, and can be a recipe for confusion.

The rules of good characterisation apply equally as well to the radio play as to other drama forms. Writers should be wary of writing main characters who are clichéd or stereotypical. A kind-hearted prostitute, an absent-minded professor, a stern-but-fair schoolteacher are examples of characters which tend to fall within these categories.

Relationships between characters can be established by the use of a word. One character referring to another as 'Darling' or as 'Sir' conveys an enormous amount of information with the minimum of fuss.

A radio play, however, may have as many minor characters as you want. A waiter might have two lines only; several diners might each have a single comment. A couple of actors with a talent for voices will play all these parts. This will sound entirely plausible and is another advantage of the medium.

Be careful of mute characters. If a character rarely speaks in a scene, then we may half forget about them. When they do speak, they then seem to jump out at us. This effect might be useful in some plays, but is usually undesirable.

DEFINITIVE VERSUS STIMULATIVE

Never try to be too specific with your descriptions. The listeners will furnish their own particular mental images for each scene – and each listener's image will be subtly different. Too much detail is dull and unwelcome – allow the listener to do some of the work. When I write the word KITCHEN, a particular set of images appear unbidden in each reader's mind. There is no need to describe a kitchen. Most people know what a kitchen is. A complex scenario has been created through the use of one word. It is always preferable to stimulate your listeners' imagination rather than restrict it.

SOUND OF HEAVY DOWNPOUR

```
3.Joanne:      Oh, the weather's awful, Jim, I'm

               soaked. It's lashing down. There's

               water everywhere. I'm wet through.

               They say that twelve inches will fall

               tonight. There's flooding in Galway

               City. Carlow's under water. I've read

               that every aircraft is grounded. My,

               is that a wave coming up the street?


4.Jim:         It's bad all right.
```

Jim couldn't have put it better. Joanne's speech would benefit from losing everything after the first sentence.

DOUBLE-ENTENDRE

Writers should be also be aware of the dreaded *double-entendre* or double meaning. Some words, while while fine in a regular dramatic work, can cause confusion in a listeners mind if you're not careful. Lines such as `What are those two for?`, `I think that ewe heard a wail` or `He was right to write down the rite` could be problematic.

IMPLICIT VERSUS EXPLICIT

Radio lends itself to intimacy, but some sensitive material must be handled as subtly as possible. Radio writers often rely more on innuendo than explicitness. A graphic lovemaking scene, for instance, could sound unintentionally hilarious.

LISTS

Beware if you find yourself writing lists – they are usually unbearably dull. Don't have one cook witter on *ad nauseam* about a favourite recipe, or have one character describe all the places they visited on a holiday.

MUSIC

If you feel that the inclusion of music is important to your play, then you can either state exactly what the piece of music is, or you can be more general. Your instruction to the producer might be:

```
SOUND: SOMBRE CLASSICAL MUSIC
```

or:

```
SOUND: 'BLUE MONDAY', SINGER FATS
DOMINO, FROM 'BLUEBERRY HILL' ALBUM.
```

RTE pays an annual fee to the Mechanical Copyright Protection Society which entitles them to play music and records. Any music or record used in your play is included in this MCPS agreement. You don't have to worry about music royalties being taken out of your fee.

If you write or perform music/songs, they can be included in your play. The producer may ask you to submit a tape with the music. The decision on whether it will be used or not is ultimately the producer's.

NARRATORS

Another common device used, if not overused, on radio is the narrator. The narrator can tell us exactly what is going on in a few lines. Several characters using dialogue might take far longer to impart the same information. This device is especially useful if you wish to hurry past a necessary though dull segment to a more interesting and vital dramatic scene.

It is often a good idea to have the narrator appear as a character in the play. If you divorce the narrator from the play's action then you could conceivably create a disjointed work. The action might stop when the narrator speaks. If the narrator has no strong connection to the story, he may not really care what happens. This ambivalence could be catching.

The narrator may be a good device if you want to place a lone character in a scene but must somehow impart essential information without recourse to dialogue. Writing what a character is thinking or having them talk to themselves can sound very artificial if clumsily handled. A narrator, on the other hand, can tell us what the character is doing or feeling.

The inclusion of a narrator and narration if used, should be kept to the bare minimum. It is usually more interesting to hear two characters talking than to have someone report what they said.

The speech below demonstrates how quickly information about time, place and circumstances can be subtly imparted to the listener. The speech contains an additional radio play device, the 'telegraph', whereby an audience knows exactly where a scene is before the scene happens at all. With the appropriate build-up beforehand, subsequent scenes can be far more dramatic and far more atmospheric.

1. Narrator: (WORKING-CLASS, ENGLISH ACCENT) I thanked God for the lack of moonlight. The Frenchies were not in a forgiving mood since the battle. Their cavalry had taken to lancing the captives. I could expect no mercy from the Hussars either – they didn't take kindly to deserters and'd string you up without thinking twice, especially if you were an infantryman. Snow was falling and I knew I had to find shelter quickly. It was then I saw the tavern's light. I made for it, hoping I'd find some gin and not an officer's sabre.

Under the speech might be the sound of wind. The next scene will undoubtedly take place in the tavern.

NUMBERS

As odd as it may seem, radio is a visual medium. Radio writers paint pictures which can be easily visualised by their audience. Avoid images which are difficult to visualise. Numbers are notoriously difficult to grasp. It's better to convey the *impression* of an object rather than its exact dimensions.

```
1.Jane:          My god, that man's as big as a hippo
```

is usually preferable to:

```
1.Jane:          My god, that man is at least two
                 metres, ten centimetres tall and must
                 weigh three dozen kilos.
```

In the same way,

```
1.Frank:         You know, in his lifetime, Postman
                 Pat must have walked 500,000 miles
```

is not as visual as:

```
1.Frank:         You know, in his lifetime, Postman
                 Pat walked so far, that he could have
                 travelled to the moon and back.
```

An audience shouldn't be expected to take notes. Give them the idea, not the statistics.

PLAY LENGTHS

One of the first limitations you will face as a radio playwright is that you must write plays of a certain length. The slots available are of fifteen minutes (for serials), 28 minutes (standard play length), 58 minutes and 88 minutes. These are the exact times; however, during normal conversation or discussions times are usually rounded off to the nearest half-hour or quarter-hour figure for convenience. The disparity is to allow time for Continuity to introduce the play and to 'back announce' it at the play's end.

It should be said that there are exceptions to every rule, and RTE has in the past broadcast plays with running times different from the above. Sometimes two short plays are broadcast back to back in order to make up a slot. While there is realistically little flexibility in the running length of these slots, there is, however, some leeway in the number of slots the writer may employ. If your work requires a long playing time, it is advisable to break it down into several episodes or parts. A six-part dramatic series consisting of 28-minute episodes is more likely to be accepted than a single radio play of 168 minutes.

It is not necessary to send in a perfectly timed script. This is practically impossible to gauge anyway; you might time your script to be 28 minutes long, but if the producer decides to increase the actors' pace then the script might come in under time. It is best to allow some margin for error. If a script is recorded and found to be one or two minutes over, the producer in post-production can usually pull it back by some judicious editing of extraneous dialogue or by shortening the gaps between the scenes. Conversely, if the play you thought was 28 minutes is a minute under, the producer might increase the gaps between scenes or have music at the beginning and end of the play. If the play is under by several minutes you may be asked to provide additional scenes.

As a rule of thumb, it is better that your script be overlong than not long enough. It is far easier to edit some lines out rather than make up some new ones in order to expand the running time of the play. An average 28-minute play runs to about 28 pages. A script submitted with 32 pages should contain an adequate safety margin. However, do not be tempted to send in a script that is vastly overwritten. The producer will not thank you for having to wade through reams of text which will ultimately have to be cut anyway. In any event, your play will usually benefit from being edited down before you submit it. You may write a page of dialogue that in your considered opinion is the greatest literary achievement ever; however, if the piece is too long or irrelevant, then it must go. There is an old writers' adage that says that you should 'murder your darlings'. It is the final play that is important, after all. No one in the audience will know if something has been edited out. You will be surprised how well your edited-down play works. If, however, you cannot stand to see a word of your text removed, then perhaps you should be writing *haiku*, not play-scripts.

PROFANITIES

The writer should be aware that profanities – so-called offensive language – are not usually considered acceptable on radio unless the play is of such significant merit that realistic dialogue is justified. The medium's intimacy ensures that a profanity takes on an exaggerated significance. You should also bear in mind that radio cannot be geared to a selective audience. A novel can be about as explicit as the writer wishes, but is unlikely to offend a reader, who is probably made aware of the book's content by the dust jacket and so voluntarily decides whether to read it or not. Radio by its nature is non-discriminatory. A radio play which is inoffensive to a car driver might embarrass a passenger. Radio characters are therefore noted for their 'Damns' and 'Blasts' rather than the more colourful equivalents.

SOUND EFFECTS

Sound effects are one of the important tools the writer has to draw on. Sound effects are usually divided into two categories: effects done live – such as a door being opened – and effects which are pre-recorded. These pre-recorded effects may be especially recorded for the play but more commonly are found on compact disc extracted from a vast library of sound effects. Just state what you want and the producer will provide it. It is not necessary to go into great detail all the time. A simple `SEASIDE SOUNDS` will be enough for the producer to go on if a setting is near the sea. You do not have to list what these sounds are; you can safely assume that the producer is familiar with the seaside. Do not worry if the exact effect you require for your play doesn't even exist. You could write a story about a mythical sea monster which cries out in pain. The ingenious producer will then come up with something appropriate – perhaps a whale sound played backwards? The sound of a Martian spaceship's hatch opening in the infamous 1938 broadcast of H.G. Welles's *War of the Worlds* (which panicked American audiences who didn't realise it was a play) was achieved by recording the lid of a jar being slowly unscrewed in a toilet bowl.

The judicious use of sound effects and acoustics can furnish a tremendous amount of information. A horse-drawn carriage passing tells us that the play is probably set in pre-industrial times; a crowded train platform informs us that it is in modern times; if there is a steam whistle then we can guess that the play is probably set sometime before 1950. If a public-address system announces that the first train for Bombay or Ballina is about to leave, we can guess the location. A sound effect or two can often furnish the audience with a better sense of time and place than a dozen lines of dialogue. In the same way, if we hear an orchestra tuning up we can probably make an educated guess at the type of character who might attend the concert. A rock band tuning up suggests a different type of character.

It should also be mentioned that sound effects should be used sparingly; they should supplement the dialogue, not replace it. Dialogue should be used to qualify the sound effects.

```
                    SOUND OF AIRCRAFT


  10.Paula:         Steady now, George. We're almost

                    there.
```

The use of the word `George` implies that the twosome are passengers in an aircraft or perhaps piloting a small plane. If we were to replace `George` with `Captain` we would conclude that the characters are piloting the aircraft. If we replace `Captain` with `Lieutenant` we could surmise that the aircraft is on a military mission.

Lists of sound effects should be avoided as they can be confusing or frustrating to listen to.

```
                    SOUND OF CAR IN DRIVEWAY

                    SOUND OF CAR DOOR OPENING AND CLOSING

                    SOUND OF FOOTSTEPS APPROACHING

                    SOUND OF KEY IN DOOR

                    SOUND OF FRONT DOOR OPENING


  11.Matthew:       My God, Jimmy, they're back already.


  12.Jimmy:         What are we waiting for? Hide.
```

If a lot of effects are required, then the careful introduction of dialogue maintains clarity.

<pre>
                        SOUND OF CAR PULLING INTO DRIVEWAY

11.Matthew: My God, Jimmy, they're back already.

                        SOUND OF CAR DOOR OPENING AND CLOSING

                        SOUND OF FOOTSTEPS APPROACHING

                        SOUND OF KEY IN DOOR

12.Jimmy: What are we waiting for? Hide.
</pre>

Don't clutter up your text by listing unnecessary sound effects. Do qualify the sound effects if the sound you desire isn't obvious; for instance, you may have in mind a scene where the opening of a door has tremendous significance. This means that the description

<pre>
        SOUND: DOOR OPENS
</pre>

probably will be inadequate. Your vision might be more aptly achieved by:

<pre>
                SOUND: HUGE DOOR OPENS WITH A LONG,

                LONG MENACING CREAK.
</pre>

Don't overdo it. Sound effects lose their impact if overused.

You should also beware of over-describing what you need. If you have a character who enters a room then all you really need to write is:

```
SOUND: DOOR.
```

There is no need for a detailed description of all the sounds associated with opening a door – the sound of a handle being pressed down and released, the door opening, the door closing, et cetera. Of course if you wish to indicate that the door is to remain open, you'd just write:

```
SOUND: DOOR OPENS.
```

Simple really. Now, to a speeding police car:

```
BRING UP INT. SPEEDING POLICE CAR


SOUND OF SIREN.
```

If you want to make it clear that the play is set in London, this isn't enough.

```
BRING UP. INT. SPEEDING POLICE CAR


SOUND OF SIREN

'BIG BEN' CHIMES IN THE DISTANCE.
```

Now we have a good idea where the play is set and what is going on, all before any of the central characters has uttered a word.

STAGE DIRECTIONS

Stage directions to the actor or producer should in the main be avoided. Remember that the actors and producers will probably have many years' experience in their respective fields – they don't need to know that

```
1.Joan:        I love you
```

should be said tenderly. If, however, it is important that a line be expressed in another way than the text suggests, you should then write in an appropriate direction such as:

```
1.Joan:        (JOKINGLY) I love you.
```

STRUCTURE

When you sit down to write your play, you should be aware of the slot you hope the finished play will be most suitable for. The first-time writer for RTE might well take on the half-hour slot as opposed to the more daunting one-hour slot. Always have in the back of your mind the intended running-length of your play. The average length of finished typed A4 script for a half-hour radio play is between 30 and 32 pages. Gauge your writing accordingly. If you have reached page 20 without yet introducing the main character, then your story is ill-paced. Save yourself a lot of hard work by mentally or physically plotting out the play. Perhaps the main characters are introduced by page 2, conflict emerges in page 3. Another problem surfaces at page 10, is solved by page 15 only to be replaced by far more significant crisis. The play reaches its climax by about page 28, everything is quickly resolved and the play is wound up by page 32.

BEGINNING THE PLAY

RTE's enormous drama output leads to a considerable demand on the recording studios. As a consequence, plays are produced in a surprisingly short space of time. A radio play might be rehearsed in the morning and recorded in the afternoon. The scripts have evolved accordingly to facilitate a speedy production schedule.

There are, broadly speaking, three categories of people looking at the same play script: the producer, the effects personnel, and the actors.

There can be no confusion about who says what, or when. The dialogue the actor has to say is clearly differentiated from the sound effects and the stage directions by a combination of *indentation, underlining, brackets, capital letters* (upper case) and *non-capital lettering* (lower case).

When your play begins, the audience is largely uncertain as to what it's going to be about. There is a potentially tremendous amount of information which the audience requires before the story can be up and running. Some schools of journalism give students a simple 'Four Ws and the H' rule to assist them when article writing. This means any article should normally provide a certain minimum of information.

- Where does the story take place?

- Who was involved?

- What happened?

- Why did it happen?

- How did it happen?

This same rule of thumb could also be applied to the radio play. We must know who is involved, what their relationships are, where the scenes take place, et cetera. Before characters and relationships are established, we must know where the play takes place.

OPENING DIRECTIONS

The first term the writer uses in a play is BRING UP. It is used at the beginning of the play and, depending on the context, at the beginning of some scenes. Some writers substitute FADE UP for BRING UP.

The next thing you must do is tell the producer the location for the scene, so that he or she can prepare the accompanying sounds. It is normal to use one or two words, three at most, to set the location, i.e. CROWDED RAILWAY PLATFORM, DESOLATE MOOR, NOISY CLASSROOM.

It is important also to specify if the scene takes place indoors or outdoors. The acoustics of each are very different. A speech delivered in a church has a different 'feel' to it than the same speech delivered outside. Write INTERIOR (INT. for short) or EXTERIOR (EXT. for short) depending on whether it is indoor or out. A typical opening direction to the producer might well be:

BRING UP.INT. SPEEDING CAR.

It is neither necessary nor desirable to add any other car sound effects, such as SOUND OF ACCELERATION, BRAKES, GEAR CHANGES and so on – it is obvious from the opening direction what is going on, and the producer will know what a speeding car sounds like. However, if there is some additional information that isn't immediately obvious, this should be included. Perhaps the car is a police car? Then a clue in dialogue or a sound effect is required.

All directions used in the play should be in CAPITALS. These directions are often indented differently from the dialogue.

```
            CUT TO EXT. CROWDED BEACH. DAY


    1.John:         (LAUGHING) I'll miss you, Annie.
```

SPACING

Dialogue, sound effects and producer's directions should be clearly separated from one another by the equivalent of *two full* double-spaces – i.e. put your typewriter on to its double-space setting and hit the 'return' key twice.

Each character's dialogue also should be clearly separated from one another and the effects by *two full* double spaces.

Separate sound effects should not be on the same line. They should be separated from one another by *one full* double space (at end of the line, click the return key once before typing the next effect).

```
            BRING UP EXT. CROWDED BEACH. DAY



                    SOUND - AN ICE-CREAM VAN

                    APPROACHES.

                    SOUND - A SEAGULL

                    SCREECHES NEARBY



    1. John:        (LAUGHING) I'll miss you, Annie.
```

You may choose to present your script in a slightly different variation to the guidelines suggested in this book. Whatever technique you employ, it is important to ensure that dialogue, sound effects, and producer's directions are clearly differentiated.

It is worth reminding yourself that great care must be taken when employing the Ws and H rule. Subtlety is the order of the day. Lines such as:

```
1.MARY:         Is that you on the green carpeted
                stairs, my darling twenty-six-year-
                old husband?
```

are fine, if the play is comic.

```
                BRING UP - INT. CAR


                SOUND: SOLEMN CHURCH BELLS NEARBY
                SOUND: CAR DOOR OPENS


1. Harry:       (QUIETLY) Are you ready, love?
```

In this sample opening there is a tremendous amount of information. The (SOLEMN) bells suggest that someone has died. Harry is obviously with someone he is close to (his 'love'), and we know that the death is of someone they know, possibly a family member or close friend, as suggested by the stage direction (QUIETLY). Harry's accent and voice would also indicate his approximate age, his social background and his nationality.

INDICATING CHARACTERS

You must clearly indicate who is speaking for the reader's benefit. The name of the character should appear in a column on the left-hand side of the page and should be underlined/made bold/capitalised for clarity. There is a gap between the character's name and the dialogue (which normally begins about a full third of a page away from the left-hand margin). This ensures that an actor won't confuse what has to be said with who has to say it. There is normally no need to write the full name of each character.

```
1. John:
```

will do instead of:

```
1. John Robinson:
```

Although it might be laborious, do not be tempted to shorten characters' names to their initials, as this can lead to confusion as well increasing your script's chances of falling into the non-user-friendly category. Avoid passages like this:

```
1. Ms M.:       Who's that?


2. JL:          It's me, your son. Bob.
```

A character's prefix, if pertinent, may be abbreviated. Some writers might write: Cpl Dobbs; Gda Murphy; Dr Spencer; Revd Hanks and so on. I personally prefer to use full titles: Corporal Dobbs; Garda Murphy, et cetera. Always use full titles in the play-text.

INDICATING SPEECHES

When the characters say anything, even if it is just one word, it is known as a *speech*. It is important that each speech is numbered. This is to allow for an expedient production; the producer can then say to an actor: 'Could you begin again, picking up from speech four on page seventeen?'

The speeches are numbered consecutively. The first speech on any new page is numbered 1. Do not continue the speech numbers to the subsequent page. It is advisable to leave the numbering until last, when you are happy with your script. The number of the speech goes on the left-hand side of the page – but well away from the edge of the paper (so it will not be covered by a binder).

INDICATING SOUND EFFECTS

Sound effects are noted simply by the word SOUND. This word covers everything heard, including music, that is not dialogue. Some writers use the term FX (shorthand for 'effects') instead, and some go even further and write SFX (spot effects) for effects which happen live, such as a door being opened, as opposed to a pre-recorded sound effect (FX), such as the sound of seagulls. The word SOUND is really sufficient. It may be used in either of two ways:

```
          SOUND: DOOR OPENS
```
or:

```
          SOUND OF DOOR OPENING.
```

Either way will do. It is important that the word SOUND comes first, that everything is in capitals and that the passages are indented correctly. This is so it cannot be confused with any other direction or dialogue.

BEGINNING AND ENDING SCENES

There are several ways of indicating the end of a scene and the beginning of another.

You may use FADE DOWN or FADE SCENE – which indicates that the scene slowly slips away and is gone a few moments after the last line. This is used when a writer wants to cement an image into the listener's mind. We hear the character's last line, and dwell on it as we hear the final fading sounds of perhaps a man crying or a woman laughing.

The next scene commences with the familiar BRING UP or FADE UP. If your last direction was FADE DOWN and the next is FADE UP, there will be an automatic moment of silence between scenes. This 'gap' is useful because it suggests that some time has passed between scenes.

As an alternative to FADE DOWN or FADE SCENE you might write CROSSFADE TO. This term is used to indicate that there is an overlap between the end of one scene and the beginning of another. This can be used to good effect if you want to counterpoint one sound directly against another; perhaps you want the sound of singing birds at the end of one scene to be heard right beside the sounds of war. This effect can also help create the illusion that the two scenes the direction bridges are occurring either simultaneously or close together.

You might also dispense with the leisurely movement from one scene to the next by writing CUT TO. This is more dramatic, more punchy. You might wish to zip from one scene in an ambulance to a house where a patient is having breathing difficulties.

If you are returning to a scene, you might use the word BACK, i.e. CROSSFADE BACK TO GARDEN; CUT BACK TO INTERIOR CASTLE MALCOLM.

There is a far simpler alternative to using CUT TOS and CROSSFADES. You can indicate the end of a scene by simply writing END OF SCENE THREE for example. You would then draw a line across the page – to separate the scenes clearly – and then write SCENE FOUR. The producer will decide which fades or cuts to use. An example might be:

```
5. MARY:        I guess we got to go, little buddy.



                    SOUND OF MOURNFUL BLEATING



END OF SCENE SEVEN

_____

SCENE EIGHT

                    INTERIOR SLAUGHTERHOUSE


6. BOB:         What do we have here then?
```

It should also be said that while you may indicate a CUT TO, the producer may decide, given the dynamics of the developing scene, that a CROSSFADE is more appropriate. Whatever terms you decide to use, stick with them for the entire play. The idea behind these terms is to avoid confusion; switching between methods defeats this purpose.

At the end of the last scene of the play you can just write FADE SCENE or FADE PLAY.

SUBMISSION LAYOUTS

A good submission is one which contains a script laid out in the appropriate format, accompanied by a couple of supplementary pages which will facilitate the reading of the script. Script readers are familiar with a set of tried and tested formats, and a script presented in a different or unusual way could conceivably distract them from properly enjoying your story.

Each submission should follow the presentation guidelines as outlined at the beginning of this book.

The drama submission itself will contain:

- a covering letter;

- a title page;

- a synopsis;

- a character listing;

- the script.

A short-story submission would contain exactly the same components, with the exception of the character listings. The title page of the short story should mention the number of words in the story.

The pages of your submission should be all fastened securely together. A staple in the left-hand corner should be perfectly adequate. A cheap slide-on plastic spine and a clear protective cover may be used if you wish. There is no need to go to the trouble or the expense of binding the manuscript.

Your submission would also include the covering letter, attached to the whole lot by a paper clip.

SPECIMEN COVERING LETTER

Editor   Josephine O'Bloggs
Arts & Drama   14 High St
Radio Centre   Castlebar
RTE   Co. Mayo
Donnybrook   Tel. (094) 12345
Dublin 4

                                              14 Sept 1995

The Editor,

Please find enclosed a 30-minute play especially
written for radio, which I hope will be considered
for broadcast. It is most suited, I believe, for
your 'Plays Peculiar' slot.

I look forward from hearing from you,

Yours sincerely

Josephine O'Bloggs.

THE COVERING LETTER

Covering letters should never exceed one page and should be as concise as possible. There is no point of going into the motivation behind the submission, why your script should be broadcast, or how much you want to hear your name on the radio. The script has to stand on its own merit. It is the script that is intended for broadcast – not your letter.

You should properly and clearly address your letter to the correct person (if known), and to the correct section. RTE has several thousand people employed both on a full-time and part-time basis; poorly addressed manuscripts can spend many weeks in an internal posting limbo as they are passed from desk to desk, getting more and more tattered in the process. When in doubt, ring RTE and ask for a name.

THE TITLE PAGE

The title page should contain:

- the name of the work;

- your full name;

- an indication if the work is a play or a story;

- the length of the play in minutes or the number of words if it's a story;

- your *permanent* address. It should be remembered that a decision from RTE can take three months or more, and if you intend moving in the meantime, they'll need to be able to contact you. Sometimes RTE may like your submission but don't have an appropriate slot for it. RTE has broadcast work submitted as long as one or two years previously. You should write your name/address prominently in the script itself in case the title page becomes separated from the script – it happens.

SPECIMEN TITLE PAGE

The Awakening

A 30-minute play for radio

by Josephine O'Bloggs

14 High St,

Castlebar,

Co. Mayo

Tel. (094) 12345

THE SYNOPSIS

The second page is normally reserved for the synopsis. The synopsis (or plot) should succinctly encapsulate the story of your play in about five or six sentences. The editor who receives the script may farm it out to an appropriate reader on the basis of your synopsis or it may be given directly to a producer who has a particular soft spot for the play's particular genre. Don't be tempted to go into all the nuances of the play – keep the synopsis short. A good tip when preparing your synopsis is to perhaps consult *The RTE Guide*, programmes usually have a two- or three-sentence 'tag' describing the programme's content. Your synopsis should be similar, it should set up the play for the reader. It should state whether the reader can expect a comedy or a serious play. The synopsis should not spoil any potential welcome surprises. If the butler did it – don't mention it here. A good synopsis will give the reader some information, but not all; it should intrigue the reader so that, curiosity aroused, he or she is keen to plunge into your script.

SPECIMEN SYNOPSIS

The Awakening is a drama and tells the story, through flashbacks, of a young girl, living on a farm, who decides that she has to run away to escape the possessive clutches of her alcoholic, widowed father.

'I gave him hell,' she says, 'and he took it all.'

It is only in later life that she comes to realise that his curt words masked a man incapable of expressing affection. She realises too, that the day he bought her a suitcase to leave home with, was probably one of the the hardest and most generous things he ever did.

CHARACTER LISTING

Each script should contain a list of the play's characters and a half-line or so about each of them. These details should include any pertinent details a producer would need to know when casting.

- The character's sex.

- The character's approximate age.

- The character's background – so that a specific actor with an affinity for the appropriate accent/traits can incorporated into the producer's mental shortlist.

There is no need overly to describe characters with minor functions.

SPECIMEN CHARACTER LISTING

<u>Characters</u>:

<u>Jill (age 13)</u> – a young Carlow girl. Shy. Angry at the world which she feels has let her down.

<u>Jill (age 40)</u> – Jill as an adult.

<u>Mikey</u> – Jill's ageing widowed father. A quiet man who's worked on a farm all his life and, in the absence of his wife, is incapable of managing his daughter.

<u>Joe (age 14)</u> – Jill's cousin – a smart alec. He often stammers when talking to Jill as he half-fancies her.

<u>Paula (age 13)</u> – Jill's best friend. From the posh side of town.

<u>A schoolteacher</u>.

<u>Several schoolgirls</u>.

SPECIMEN SCRIPTS

The following two specimen play extracts use slightly different layouts. You should pick 'n' mix the methods and choose the best combination for yourself and your typewriter/processor. Whatever system you decide on, stick with it for the whole play.

It should also be pointed out that the samples used in this book are proportionally correct only – an A4 page is significantly larger than these pages.

SPECIMEN SCRIPT#1

<u>A SERVANT OF TWO MASTERS</u>   Page #1

FADE UP INTERIOR - AN ULTRA HI-

TECH PLUSH LIFT

FX: SYNTHESISED

SUPERMARKET 'MUZAK'

FX: LOW BACKGROUND HUM OF

'EVELYN'

FX: ELECTRONIC FLOOR

INDICATOR - 'DING DONG'

FX: DOORS SLIDE OPEN WITH

AN EFFICIENT 'SHUSH'

A SERVANT OF TWO MASTERS   Page #2

'EVELYN' REPRESENTS THE LATEST

IN COMPUTER SYNTHESISATION. IT

HAS THE VOICE OF A SENSUAL

WOMAN AND IS DESIGNER-SULTRY –

THE SORT OF SEXY PURR THAT

EXISTS ONLY IN FANTASY.

SHE SHOULD SOUND REAL, NOT

'ELECTRONIC'

1. Evelyn: (*FROM SPEAKERS IN THE LIFT. PURRS*) We

have arrived at Floor Six. (*PAUSE*)

Haberdashery. Have a nice day.

(*PAUSE*)

                    FX: DOOR INDICATOR

Mind the doors please. Mind the

doors.

                    FX: DOOR CLOSES

(*PAUSE, SUGGESTIVE*) Descending.

AFTER A FEW MORE MOMENTS

FX: DOOR INDICATOR

FX: DOORS OPEN

1. <u>Evelyn</u>:   We have arrived at Floor Five.

(**PAUSE**) Sports and Leisure. Tally-ho,

boys. (**PAUSE**) Mind the doors please.

Do mind the doors.

FX: DOOR INDICATOR

FX: DOORS CLOSE

Descending.

2. <u>Evans</u>:   (**MANAGING DIRECTOR. SELF-MADE**

MILLIONAIRE. LEFT SCHOOL IN HIS EARLY

TEENS) Remarkable.

3. <u>Davison</u>:   (**YOUNG CAREER EXECUTIVE**) Thank you,

sir.

A SERVANT OF TWO MASTERS   **Page #4**

1. <u>Evans</u>:   I'm impressed.

2. <u>Davison</u>:   Thank you again.

3. <u>Evans</u>:   I would say another pay rise is in order for the work you've done. Gambol & Blooms has never looked better.

4. <u>Davison</u>:   It's nothing.

5. <u>Evans</u>:   No, Davison. Don't dismiss your achievements. The store has never looked better. Your ideas for the colour schemes in Lingerie, Ladies-Wear and Electrical Goods were incisive. The decor in DIY was inspired and regarding the fittings in the management boardrooms – sensational.

A SERVANT OF TWO MASTERS   **Page #5**

1. <u>Evans</u>:   (**CONT.**) This was a sick building.
There was the smell of must in the
executive washroom.

2. <u>Davison</u>:   You are too kind, sir. Too kind. Ah.
Almost at our floor now, sir.

CUT TO INT. SMALL ROOM

*FX: CLANK OF NEARBY LIFT
MACHINERY*

3. <u>Potter</u>:   (**ELDERLY MAN. TO HIMSELF**) That's what
you think, boyos.

CUT BACK to INT. LIFT

4. <u>Evelyn</u>:   We have arrived at Floor Seven.
General Administration. Keep typing,
girls. Have a nice day. Mind the

1. Evelyn: (**CONT.**) doors please. Mind the doors.

2. Evans: Remarkable. Used to work on an 0898
                  adult phone line you say?

3. Davison: Yes, sir. We auditioned several
                  hundred women just to get the right
                  voice for the computer.

4. Evans: And whose voice is it? I should like
                  to meet her.

5. Davison: Pardon my choice of words, sir. Like
                  the back of a bus. Hasn't got a tooth
                  in her head. Balding into the
                  bargain. She's sixty if she's a day.

6. Evans: Tragedy, Evans, a tragedy.

7. Davison: With a capital T, sir.

SPECIMEN SCRIPT #2

<u>THE MONEY PIT</u>

SCENE ONE

LONG ECHOING MINESHAFT

<u>WATER DRIPS</u>

<u>MUFFLED SEA POUNDS AGAINST</u>

<u>SHAFT WALL</u>

<u>SOUND OF SHOVEL DIGGING</u>

1. NARRATOR/JOHN: (<u>A CANADIAN IN HIS FORTIES. HE IS</u>

<u>DEATHLY TIRED. HE COUGHS/WHEEZES</u>

<u>FREQUENTLY IN THE FOUL AIR AND DUST</u>)

One inch more, Martha. And one inch

less to go. How many inches has that

been today, Martha? This week? Too

many, Martha, to count.(<u>COUGHS, SINGS</u>

<u>ROUGHLY</u>) 'Sixteen men on a dead man's

chest.' (<u>COUGHS</u>) Can't be much longer

(1)

THE MONEY PIT

1. JOHN: (<u>CONTINUED</u>) now. 'Yo ho ho and a
              bottle -' (<u>COUGHS</u>) I'll make it up to
              you. (<u>WEARILY</u>) To you both. Argh!

                      <u>SPADE SNAPS SUDDENLY AND</u>
                      <u>CLATTERS TO THE GROUND</u>
                      <u>JOHN IN EXHAUSTION FALLS</u>
                      <u>HEAVILY AND AWKWARDLY,</u>
                      <u>HURTING HIMSELF</u>

              (<u>ALMOST IN TEARS</u>) Damned spade.
              Blasted spade. Let me down. You've
              all let me down. Away, damn you.

                      <u>SPADE HURLED AWAY</u>

              (<u>SOBS</u>) Away. A curse on you. On you
              all. Oh, that I ever set eyes on this
              Godforsaken island.(<u>PAUSE. BOUT OF</u>
                          (2)

THE MONEY PIT

1. JOHN: (CONTINUED. COUGHING. SINGS, SLOWLY

                GENTLY) 'Row, row, row your boat,

                gently down the stream ...'

                END OF SCENE ONE

_____

                SCENE TWO

                ON THE OPEN SEA. SUMMER'S DAY

                        SEAGULLS

                        SOUND OF SMALL BOAT BEING

                        ROWED

                JOHN, MARTHA – HIS WIFE – AND THEIR

                TEN-YEAR-OLD SON, JAMES, ARE ENJOYING

                THEMSELVES TREMENDOUSLY. JAMES IS

                ROWING. ALL THREE GAILY SING 'ROW,

                ROW, ROW YOUR BOAT'. SOON ...

                        (3)

THE MONEY PIT

1. BOY: (<u>BREATHLESS</u>) How am I doing, Papa? My
               arms aren't tired – not one bit.

2. MARTHA: Oh, look at him. My son the sailor!

3. BOY: Why, I must have rowed a league and a
               half.

4. JOHN: Nay. Two leagues. I'm certain of it.

5. MARTHA: Why, at this rate you'd be able to
               carry us all the way to London and
               still be back in Nova Scotia for
               supper.

6. BOY: (<u>BREATHLESS</u>) I think perhaps I'll let
               you take over now, Papa.

7. MARTHA: So do you still want to be a sailor
               now?

                        (4)

THE MONEY PIT

1. BOY: Oh yes, please. May I come with you,
               please, Papa? Next time?

2. JOHN: Only if you are well. Only if you are
               well.

               END OF SCENE TWO

───

               SCENE THREE

               QUIET ROOM.

                    CLOCK TICKS

                    A PONY AND TRAP PASS BY

                    OUTSIDE

3. MARTHA: Well, Doctor?

4. DOCTOR: I'm sorry.
                    (5)

<u>THE MONEY PIT</u>

1. MARTHA: Oh no, no.

2. JOHN: Easy, Martha, easy.

               END OF SCENE THREE

_____

               SCENE FOUR

               BOAT NEAR SEASHORE

3. BOY: Here we are. Papa, Mama, here we are.
               I told you I would make it. I'm not
               sick. I told you.

4. MARTHA: (<u>SADLY</u>) Yes, we knew you could.
               You're not sick. Not at all.

               END OF SCENE FOUR

_____

               (6)

SERIAL SCRIPT LAYOUTS

The essential differences between the layout of a serial and the layout of a regular play is that the serial script tends to have a far simpler format.

A daily serial leads to considerable pressure on producers and production facilities. Producers tend to favour a far more streamlined script then the usual playscript. Directions such as CROSSFADE or FADE UP/DOWN are dispensed with in favour of a universal CUT TO. Sound effects are often indicated simply by FX. In serials such as *RiverRun,* a passage might well be:

```
           CUT TO HAPPY GARDENS RESTAURANT.


               FX: PARTY IN PROGRESS


  1. Terry:     What are you doing here?


  2. Patrick:   I might ask you the same question.


               CUT TO EXT. STREET.


  3. Brenda:    Hurry up, will you? I've simply loads
               to tell.
```

There is no need to mention the type of restaurant Happy Gardens is. Presumably the producer will be eminently familiar with this location, and such descriptions will therefore be superfluous.

WRITING RADIO SHORT STORIES

Short stories written for radio are subtly different than those written for magazines or book collections. Stories written for radio will be read aloud by a reader, probably an actor, and a good story therefore will take account of this. Remember, people reading need to breathe too, and those breathing points should fall upon natural breaks in the text indicated by the commas or full stops. You can easily read a sentence which may contain many dozens of words; such a sentence, however, is not easily read aloud. The solution therefore is to write short sentences or phrases, using lots of commas or dashes to break up your text.

Listeners hear the words spoken and care should be taken that words which look well on paper are radio-friendly – beware the *double-entendre* or double meaning: Ah I see there's my buoy too causes problems as does I heard the baby wail.

Short-story writers who write for publication have one luxury that radio short-story writers do not – they can write down long, meandering and complex thoughts and descriptions, sprinkled with obscure words or terminology. If a reader has a problem with a passage then they will reread the piece and tease it out; if there's a problematic word, they might perhaps reach for a dictionary. Listeners have no such control of the story; they cannot go back if there is an unclear passage. Radio short stories should be less obtuse then their magazine counterparts. Images should be clear, and descriptions exact and correct.

Radio short stories also break away from the usual writer's convention where you are not supposed to describe something in two words when one will do. In radio stories you can and do often describe the same thing several times in different ways. This is to reinforce important points which might be missed otherwise.

```
It was a truck, a great big truck, all red and
shiny, and I loved it.
```

Radio is a very intimate medium, and a good short story told by an actor has greater impact if the impression is given that the story actually happened to the person reading the story. A popular radio short-story device is therefore one where use is made of the first person. 'I did it' can be more powerful than 'He did it'. To reflect this intimacy, stories may be of an intimate, personal nature and told using the speech and syntax of real speech. A radio short story is a grammarian's nightmare as sentences are disjointed, left hanging, et cetera.

Radio short stories are written to be read aloud; the approach should be to write something in a style similar to the one you might use when talking to a close silent friend about a very personal moving moment. This is an extract from a broadcasted radio short story, called 'Birth Mark', by writer Claire Keegan.

```
We are laid out here on our white beds waiting
for them to come and take away our lunch trays.
The lady opposite has two green, glass eyes
which she keeps immersed in some kind of
solution. She puts them in while Gloria is
offering me a grape. Gloria looks across and
sees her and then looks at the grape in her
hand. We are not able to stop giggling. I know
that neither of us will ever again be able to
see a grape without thinking of this lady with
the glass eyes.
```

I am in for a C-section. My belly is a hard mound beneath the sheets. There are complications; the baby is breach. They will not risk what they call a 'normal delivery' because of what happened last time. So they are going to slice open my belly and take the baby out through the opening. They told me this in low voices as if they were urging me to cheat at some game. Instead, I should be lying on my back with my legs up, making dough out of my husband's hand, watching them extract the infant out of my body with a forceps. Only the weak use drugs. If pain had a memory, nobody in her right mind would have more than one baby. Women are lunatics. I am here, subjecting myself to their knives. The thought is enough to make me feel that I will never again be aroused.

I'm doing this because the last one died. The day we buried her, it was like playing a burial game. We had a child-sized coffin - a little white one with brass handles, the real thing; a child-sized hole in the ground, a child-sized corpse, and lots and lots of people there who never knew the child. Including me. The priest didn't want to bury her in the graveyard because she wasn't baptised, so I made up this cock-and-bull story about putting her head under the tap and baptising her myself. He asked me what name had I given her and I said the very first thing that popped into my head: 'Abigail.'

'Abigail what?' he asked me.

'Just Abigail,' I said. Dead girls don't need names. There's no one to call in to tea, to stand up when the roster is read out. So they put that name, Abigail, on the child-sized headstone.

I'm not going to give this one a name. I'm leaving it all up to Frank. What a laugh that is. He's at home watching the telly. I'm the one who's in here, waiting. I'm the one they'll cut open and make two of. If I'm lucky. The blind lady had her baby girl last night and I think there must be something wrong with it. She's been silent ever since her husband came in, curled up like a rope. She can't even cry. You'd never think to look at her that she was ever pregnant, she's so trim. I'd love to be her. Nothing ever prepared me for this. The only thing my mother told me about having babies was that you'd be dying for a cup of tea afterwards, and when you got it, it was the best cup of tea in the world. She had six of them. Now I'm stuck here in a room full of expanded women and pink carnations and blue irises and ugly babies. I'm terrified.

It has begun too soon. It started slowly, like
an oven door opening and closing inside of me.
I don't tell anyone. Instead, I keep my head
down and look at no one - as if seeing no one
will make me invisible. I stay like this for a
long time and then that oven door turns into
something else. The shock waves slide through
my body now, and the heat intensifies,
contracts. Rhythms wash into me, several
different types of terrible music, and I want
to get up and dance them out of me. I try to
move. They form knots in my abdomen, they push
down into my rectum and their strains are
getting bigger, tighter. They are stronger than
I. They twist, are too big for me to contain,
so I get up and stumble around the room trying
to dance, thinking I will have some chance if I
go with them. And now there's this silly nurse
beside me wearing a white, folded napkin on her
head and she's telling me to breathe. 'Breathe!
Breathe!' she says as if breathing is something
I would not ordinarily do. I am the Gordian
Knot and they will come and slice me with their
swords. This is my last thought before the
darkness descends over me.

On paper your short story might look dreadful, full of hyphens, commas, and
whatever – but that doesn't matter. It's meant only to *sound* attractive.

FEATURES & DOCUMENTARIES

Writing Features and Documentaries. Submission
Tips. Submission Layouts.

Features & Documentaries is the result of a recent restructuring within RTE. This grouping is responsible for 22 programmes which include *Soundbyte, The Sunday Show*, all education programmes, all religious programmes, afternoon programmes such as the game show *Panel Beaters*, the Wednesday documentary, *The Live Register*, most of Saturday and Sunday-evening programming up until nine o'clock, and all daytime and evening features and documentary output. Documentaries and features therefore represent a significant percentage of Radio One's programming.

These programmes could be one-offs or they could form a series. They are normally broadcast only on Radio One. The slots for the programmes may vary and their places in the schedules depend on a combination of the programme's contents and the slot availability.

You should be relieved to know that there is considerable interaction between the various producers, and that there are no clearly defined departments. The offices of the Radio Centre are large and open-plan. A drama producer is likely to have a desk right beside a features producer, and so submissions which a producer feels are inappropriate for themselves could be informally passed to someone more suitable. This informality is useful for programmes which require cooperation between the areas. One such category, the so-called drama-documentary (a documentary which include re-creations of events played by actors as a substitute for the sometimes dull presentation of bald facts), is of special interest to Managing Editor of Features & Arts, Michael Littleton.

> I am interested in seeing drama-documentaries developed in a modern way, which would possibly involve actors playing non-existent voices, voices from the past or whatever – in a marriage between that and existing material. For instance, in the RTE archives you would have the voices of people like Austin Clarke. You wouldn't be able to tell the Austin Clarke story just by using what's there from him, but what you could do is use biographical information to back up your material and this could be articulated into scenes played by actors. You could use his own voice as well combined with these scenes. It would literally be drama-documentary – it would not be a documentary written in purely a dramatic form but a marriage of dramatic art and documentary art. I'd like to see that developed. If anyone has ideas along that line then then they can be explored. There is another thing to be said. There are more ways than one of making a drama-documentary; however I'm not so keen on getting in scripts on, say, *David Copperfield* on some anniversary of the author where the whole thing is cast out in fairly simple form. That kind of documentary isn't of all that much of an interest. We have done very few of them. They can be very difficult and time-consuming. They require good writing plus a knowledge of where you can get hold of old tapes and things of that kind which would fill out the artistic proportions of a programme. Kevin O'Connor did one for me

some years ago called *The Sieges of Limerick* – there was more than one siege. He discussed the reconstruction in Limerick and the discovery of the old walls in a modern context with historians, and in between recreated some of the battle scenes. He dramatised aspects of people's lives from that era, such as their pastimes. He included what they ate and drank and what the price of things were. He succeeded, in other words, in mixing drama with historical and geographical fact. That's a form of documentary which is underused, possibly because it's too difficult and possibly because we never actually focused on it. There is no reason why you should be restricted by a lack of material dealing with past events; you can bring in dramatised forms. You don't have to do it purely as a drama script or using interviews with experts – you can marry the two formats. I would hope to encourage some of that in the future.

It remains to be seen which radio grouping (Arts & Drama or Features & Documentaries) will take overall responsibility for this category of programming.

Features & Documentaries covers a comprehensive range of programming and is probably the best home for any idea which is not clearly a play, short story or an idea with an arts theme, all of which should be sent to Arts & Drama.

Appropriate submissions should be clearly addressed to: The Commissioning Editor, Features & Documentaries, Radio Centre, RTE, Donnybrook, Dublin 4.

WRITING FEATURES AND DOCUMENTARIES

Most of the programmes broadcast on the RTE network are initiated and produced by RTE's in-house producers. However, an increasingly significant amount of output is suggested by freelance presenters. In recognition of this, RTE have appointed a new commissioning editor who will assist freelance programme-makers.

RTE have a policy of assigning a producer to all submissions earmarked for development. If you submit an idea which is accepted, you will have considerable producing input into the proposed programme – it was your idea after all. However, there will always be an RTE person, known as perhaps the producer, the executive producer, or series producer, responsible for the programme. Even a submission by a highly experienced ex-RTE producer would normally be assigned someone. This policy is to ensure that submissions are up to broadcast standard and that the programmes are suitable for broadcast. RTE, as the state broadcaster, has to ensure that whatever goes out on its network is legal and complies with all broadcasting rules, regulations and restrictions.

The policy also recognises the reality that many people with good ideas often don't have the technical know-how to put them into practice.

> If somebody from the outside comes with a good idea and it is decided to go with that idea, technicians are assigned to work on the programme and there is also a producer assigned to work with people on programmes to guide them through it. That has worked very well and has always been the practice. We're there to show them the pitfalls, not to do the work for them, because

sometimes there would be a danger that a good idea could be taken over and the person's enthusiasm would be blunted very seriously. We will guide the person along and if we see them making a mistake we say, 'Don't do that,' and explain to them why. I mean we're aware that if people are not practised at using microphones, if they are not practised at editing and don't know the terminology of radio, the shorthand which we take for granted, then they can get lost and intimidated very easily.

Paddy Glackin, Editor Features & Documentaries

It is very helpful to have the support of an experienced producer, for, once the tapes are in, the shape of the programme could be very different from that originally envisaged. The focus of interest might have shifted; perhaps what you thought would be a nugget is anything but. You should not be entirely surprised at this – your initial plan might bear little relevance to the recorded material and this is quite common. It can easily happen that an interview subject, normally the most talkative person in the world, suddenly clams up and becomes monosyllabic when a microphone is placed on the table in front of him or her.

A person who makes a programme for radio broadcast often fulfils several roles. For practical purposes, the term 'presenter' is used (unless indicated otherwise) for the rest of this chapter to mean the person who submitted the idea, while 'producer' refers to the RTE person assigned to assist them.

A freelance presenter can be anyone with a story. This story should be something which will be of interest to others. It can be about anything you like, and if RTE approves of the idea then you can be in it yourself. There is no union requirement for documentary-making. All it requires is a good idea, enthusiasm and a willingness to see ideas through.

You don't have to have a BA or an M.Litt. to be able to communicate on the radio. Not everybody is a broadcaster, and it's like writing books: you may only have one book in you, you may only have one programme in you, and that might be it. I'd certainly be more than open to giving somebody a shot at making a programme. I know that in the last three years, I think we've used certainly two dozen new people, some of whom would have just one documentary, some of whom would have done one series, and some who have done several series or several documentaries.

John McKenna, Producer

A good idea for a documentary need not be something huge or dramatic – you may be the chairwoman of the *Titanic* Commemoration Society brimming with lots of dramatic material about the subject, or you may be a football player talking about an impending final. A good documentary is one which delivers information in a new, interesting or refreshing way. A good documentary-maker can tell a good story well. If you can't tell a good story in an engaging fashion, you will make a potentially fascinating topic dull.

A documentary takes a long time to make when you take into account the time taken in working out a plan of the idea, gathering material, recording it, editing it and so on. It is therefore important, for your own sanity, that your subject is something that will carry you over the weeks. Enthusiasm will help you over the long hours. The ideal subject should be something you know. You might think that a documentary about spot-welding will be of tremendous interest – and if told in an entertaining fashion it could well be – but if you don't know the first thing about it, you'll find yourself spending long, often wearisome hours in research. Chances are you will become fed up along the way and quietly let the matter drop.

It should also be said that if you're constantly sending in ideas and never following any of them through, you will develop a justifiably poor track record. This certainly won't aid your chances of getting a proper hearing on a subject that would normally stand a good chance of getting developed.

Once the editor is satisfied that you have a feasible idea, he or she may ask for a more detailed outline including budgetary details, interview subjects and how you intend to proceed. If actors are to read segments, those pieces should be included, and if copyrighted, permission should be sought. You may then be commissioned to make the documentary.

It should also be mentioned that at present the decision to commission a programme or series of programmes is made on the basis of a 'paper' submission, often combined with an informal discussion with the proposer of the project. Paddy Glackin intends to amend the system somewhat. The programme proposer will still have to make a paper submission, but the next stage could well be the production of a 'pilot' programme – especially useful for testing the viability of a series.

> I would hope to put far greater emphasis on pilot programming so that we can hear what the thing actually sounds like. When you hear a pilot programme you can then make suggestions as to how to make it better, whereas if you just go away and do something and then commit it from paper to tape and then put it put on air, you're removing the safety net and that can be very dangerous.
>
> *Paddy Glackin, Editor Features & Documentaries*

S U B M I S S I O N   T I P S

So you are interested in doing a documentary. What's the first step? Find an idea that you believe would make good radio, something that would be of interest to RTE listeners. Then check it out by doing some tentative research. Go to the library and read a little on the topic; talk informally to a few people who might make good interview subjects. If the idea still seems sound, the next stage is to write a submission. There are a couple of rules of thumb when preparing a submission.

• Try to approach the subject from an interesting, unusual angle, and remember that the programme is about its *subject* – not about you. Some of the best documentaries feature interviews where the interviewer has been entirely edited out, so that the entire focus was on the interviewee.

• Don't try to pack too much material into a single programme.

• Decide on the central issue and concentrate on that.

Producer John McKenna has this advice:

> I think that the basis of any good radio programme is telling a story, whatever that story might be, and the closer you can get to the person about whom the story is being made, the better. In other words, the less the presenter is there the better, and the more of the story that's there the better.

Programme budgets are not huge. To illustrate, someone who successfully submits and presents a 43-minute documentary, for example, can expect to receive a fee of about £600. This is not a tremendous amount of money when you take into account all the hours which may go into producing the programme. There would be additional monies for the programme's budget, but these are finite. A submission with an unrealistic budget is unlikely to be approved. Programmes which require extensive international travelling will be examined closely but would have to possess substantial merit to be seriously considered. Anyone preparing a submission should 'guesstimate' the costs of the programme. Costs might include travel, overnight accommodation, copyright payments, 'hospitality', actors' fees (if dramatic work is used), musicians' fees, stationery, batteries for the recorder, tape, etc. It is usually not necessary to include in the programme's budget the salary of the RTE personnel involved or the hire of RTE facilities (studios or portable recording equipment).

There are two key points documentary makers should be aware of.

- Make sure you can get permission to make the programme. A programme about a particular writer may be refused permission to use book/play extracts by the publishers; a proposal to make a documentary on a visiting 'superstar' could be impossible without the person's and/or their management's permission; a 'behind the scenes' documentary on the making of a proposed big-budget movie is not feasible if the film producer thinks you're going to clutter up the set.

- Don't be obvious in your choice of subject. A proposed programme on a major forthcoming event such as the Eurovision Song Contest will probably be adequately covered.

Your proposal should consist of a covering letter and a project outline. The letter should be concise – avoid going beyond a page if you can. The letter should state what you want to do, why you want to do it, why you think it should be done and why you should be the one to do it. It is also advisable to include any relevant experience you have, however minuscule.

Your submission idea should be sent to: Commissioning Editor Features & Documentaries, Radio Centre, RTE, Donnybrook, Dublin 4.

INTERVIEW TIPS

You should know what you intend to achieve by the interview and prepare questions accordingly.

- Know your interviewee. Find out as much as you can about him or her before the interview – this background material can be helpful in preparing questions and asking unscripted questions.

- Prepare a good interview environment. Few people will open up if they can be overheard. Some people would be more relaxed meeting in a pub, others in a coffee shop, others at home.

- Check recording equipment before you meet. It can be very off-putting if you're inserting batteries and cassettes, and testing the mike *ad nauseam* in the presence of your subject. You should make a quick sound-check just before the interview in order to check on recording levels and the presence or absence of extraneous noise.

- Always carry spare batteries and tape. A friend of mine – a journalist – had, to her considerable embarrassment, to re-record an interview several days later because the batteries died a few minutes into the interview.

- Use good interview techniques. Nod your head to encourage the subject to speak – don't say 'ahuh, ahuh' or finish their sentences. You can't be edited out if you're talking over someone.

- When interviewing, use a good mounted mike. If you use a hand mike, move it back and forth between you in a smooth, even fashion during the interview. A tip is to maintain eye contact – your subject will be less drawn to the wavering microphone if you look each other in the eye.

- Ask the questions you'd planned, but do be prepared to ask other questions which suggest themselves during the interview.

Documentaries by their nature are not predictable, and no one knows if they've a good documentary recorded until they've listened to the tapes. You need to be tolerant and flexible. An interviewee might not show up, but the person who delivered the message might furnish a mother lode of material. Each documentary is different. One person speaking into a microphone uninterrupted for an hour could be riveting, while another documentary may require lots of inserts, sound effects, actors reading pieces and more. The tendency today is to concentrate on human-interest stories, stories which have an attractive sound ambience. Michael Littleton, Managing Editor Features and Arts, however, points out that there are plenty of programmes which provide informational segments, and therefore a radio documentary should veer away from the cold delivery of facts. A radio documentary should have an interesting, perhaps eclectic, style which draws in the listener.

> Generally we like to convey something rather than tell it in a documentary. *Dreaming of Fat Men* [a documentary by Lorelei Harris], had no narration whatever in it, yet the story was told as if there was a narrator. It told a whole lot of facts about food fanatics, it told a whole lot though about human interest, about how addicts behave when they get together and talk more freely to each other. It gave an insight into the world of people who are worried about overeating and about food and about their own sense of self-respect, which, was in my opinion, both painful in parts and humorous at the same time. I cannot remember how many proposals we've had to do programmes on that kind of thing that I have rejected, but mostly it was because they were very obvious – tables of facts, dietitian's narration, so on and so forth. That is a perfectly proper broadcast to make, but it isn't the way we're trying to move the documentary output.

SUBMISSION LAYOUTS

Apart from good presentation and the appropriate layout, Documentaries & Features appreciate an additional quality in the submissions they receive – namely, brevity. Try to encapsulate your ideas as concisely as possible. Your initial submission should number several pages, not several dozen. Arts & Drama expect complete scripts, Features & Documentaries expect complete ideas. If the idea has merit, you'll be contacted and asked for further detailed information. This is the point when you go into specifics.

A submission which includes dramatic material should use the appropriate 'play-script' layout. If your submission is to contain dramatised material, it is usually sufficient to include a sample scene or two.

You have two priorities. One is to adequately convey a good, realistic idea; the second is to demonstrate that you are capable of effectively carrying through that idea.

THE COVERING LETTER

The covering letter should be brief and to the point. The editor needs only to know who you are, what the subject is, why you want to do it and whether you have any relevant experience, no matter how trivial.

The latter is very important. A good idea is only as good as the person who carries it out. It is advisable to gain some experience of the radio medium, perhaps by doing some volunteer work for a local independent radio station or a hospital in-house radio programme. Such experience will help demonstrate your capability, while the experience will give you invaluable insights into the requirements and capabilities of radio, enhancing in turn your submission.

SPECIMEN COVERING LETTER

```
Editor                              John McCartin
Features & Documentaries            12 The Heights
Radio Centre                          Castlebridge
RTE                                    Co. Kildare
Donnybrook                      Tel. (055) 21329
Dublin 4

                                    1 August 1995

The Editor,

I am writing to you as I believe that I have an idea
for a documentary that you might be interested in.

It would be about our local priest. Before he
arrived in the area, I was signing on and becoming
involved in petty crime - now I'm in a band and
having a whale of a time.

Father John has also said that he will be pleased to
participate in this project - he says that it might
be the ideal forum to launch our new single.

I believe that I would be well able to organise and
present such a documentary. I am comfortable with
interview techniques, having worked with North East
Radio for a summer as a reporter for Up and Coming -
a weekly live music review programme. I've also been
presenting a hospital in-house radio show for two
years now.

I've enclosed a rough outline of what I think the
documentary could look like.

Yours sincerely,


John McCartin.
```

THE OUTLINE

The outline should be crisp, focused and written in a way that demonstrates that you have thought through your idea. A commissioning editor must be able to easily visualise what you hope to achieve. A good outline will indicate if the documentary is feasible and if there is a danger of overloading the programme with too much material. A good outline should contain all pertinent information, including details such as:

- how long the documentary will take to make;

- how many people will be required to be in it;

- the programme's angle. Will the entire programme be studio based? Will the approach be comic? Will dramatic reconstructions be used?

It will also contain sufficient details to allow the editor to estimate how much the documentary will eventually cost. A detailed budget is not really required at this stage. Exceptional costs, however, if they are vital to the programme, should be included and justified.

The outline itself should come to only a couple of pages. It is impossible to map out too precisely any proposed documentary. You might have lots of ideas for elaborate set-ups – recording in underground passages, interviewing people on ships, talking to people in a local pub. It might look splendid on paper but when you record, you might discover that you have an interview subject who is so compelling that everything has to be abandoned in favour of a single voice speaking for a powerful 45 minutes.

If the commissioning editor likes the idea, he or she will contact you. No commissioning editor is going to guarantee you a slot on the basis of an enquiry. You may be required to furnish further information such as: what would you require from RTE? What help would you need? What equipment? Do you have your subject's permission? Can you get it? And so on.

SPECIMEN OUTLINE

Outline of proposed 28-min. documentary –

working title 'The Black Sheep'

The documentary would cover a three-week period between band rehearsals to recording of demo record planned to take place on 10 November.

The documentary opens with sound of a rock group tuning up.

Then there is the sound of church organ.

Presenter (myself) speaks, asking, 'What is it that connects both sounds? It's a priest, Father John.'

The documentary would feature snippets on various members of the band, such as lead singer Paula, for example. She could discuss her background, how she was unemployed and had left home at thirteen without a job, what her hopes are for group, et cetera.

We'd also hear extracts of the band preparing for their first gig on 3 September, which is to pay for the studio hire to make the demo record.

It will be a no-holds-barred fly-on-the-wall type documentary. No doubt there'll be some friction in the group – some are getting stage fright, some still vehemently disagree with the present name, 'The Black Sheep'. The bass player has said he's thinking of going to England; we'll be in a fix if he does. Throughout the programme we'd feature snippets of John's comments, his hopes for us and so on.

The last thing we'd hear would be the demo record, which would also simultaneously be our big break on the national airways.

THE FEATURE/DOCUMENTARY SCRIPT

Feature/documentary scripts are not required in the initial submission; in fact it would be impossible to put together a complete draft before recordings are complete.

When a documentary has been commissioned, it is vital that you keep an adequate log of the recordings. Label each tape clearly, indicating what it contains and the duration of the recording. At some point it will be necessary to go into an RTE studio to record inserts and to edit the tape. It is vital that you are adequately prepared so that you can ensure that the editing/recording process goes as quickly and efficiently as possible.

When studio time arrives, tapes containing material needed should be pre-set to the relevant section, actors' scripts (if necessary) should be ready for use, your personal script should be rehearsed and prepared, compact discs for the music inserts should be under your arm and cuts on tapes should be clearly indicated.

A clear script format is required to indicate to the producer and the technicians which music inserts are needed, where and how long they'll be, what speech goes in and what is cut. The script given here is an example of one particular format. The producer will of course assist you in the preparation of a recording script and will have assembled much of the material – such as music from the archives – on your behalf. A recording script should give you some indication of the administration behind a programme – there's more to making a documentary than recording, there's tapes to be logged, scripts to be researched and typed.

An efficient, well-prepared recording script is one that could be quickly made into a finished documentary by the producer, technicians, actors and so on, without you present.

SPECIMEN STUDIO SCRIPT

The 'Black Sheep'
A documentary.

Presenter/Researcher – John McCartin. **Producer** – Jenny Kelly. **Sound Engineer** – Frank Duffy. **Sound Supervision** – n/a

Tape length – 28 minutes. **Transmission Date** – to be decided.

Suggested Continuity Intro: 'Now a programme which traces the emergence of a young band from their early days until their debut single. RTE presents The Black Sheep.'

Time	Pre-set/Studio/Insert	Duration
00.	TAPE 4B (Recording of band practice)	30 Secs.
00.30	COMPACT DISC – (BBC Sound Effects CHURCH ORGAN)	15 Secs
00.45	PRESENTER/STUDIO	10 Secs

A band tuning up, church bells.

What exactly do these things

have in common? Not a lot, you

1

<u>Time</u>	<u>Pre-set/Studio/Insert</u>	<u>Duration</u>

(CONT.) might think, but nothing
could be further from the truth.
The answer is a band - The Black
Sheep. Why Black Sheep? Because
it somehow, at least at the
time, seemed so fitting. We all
came from different backgrounds,
but we all had something in
common.

0.55	TAPE 2C.	2.10

Interview with Paula, lead singer

Pick up 'Me, oh I don't know'

End - 'well, wish me luck.'

3.05	TAPE 8A	10

Band practice.

3.15	TAPE 9C	1.50

Interview with Father John.

2

Time	Pre-set/Studio/Insert	Duration
	P/U. 'I think we've created ...'	
	End - 'So what do you reckon?'	
4.55	TAPE 4B.	1.25
	Interview with bass-player,	
	Pick up 'Two-Chord-Charlie,	
	they called me ...'	
	End - 'give it a lash.'	
5.20	PRESENTER/STUDIO	4

When I first told me Ma that I
had a job, she was delighted.
When I told her it was with the
help of the new parish priest
she said she'd drop him a little
extra in the collection plate.
When I told her it was a band I
was in, she launched into what
became the first of many decades
of the rosary.

3

PART III

TELEVISION & FILM

FILM AND TV WRITING

Useful Terms and Terminology. Writing Film. Writing
TV Drama. Writing Soaps. Writing Documentaries.
Writing Comedy. Writing Animation. Writing
Advertising.

If there is one fact that potential television screenwriters should know, it is that
television production is expensive – very expensive. A half-hour home-
produced drama can easily cost around £50,000 to make. It is no surprise that
RTE's main 'soaps' – *Glenroe* and *Fair City* – soak up practically all of its
television drama budget, leaving it with little resources for much other 'in-
house' drama. This commercial reality means that substantial dramatic
productions are likely to be produced by two or more partners. RTE has
produced dramatic work with other television stations, such as the BBC, and
this pattern is likely to continue.

Of course, television isn't all about drama; there are documentaries, game
shows, children's programmes and more. These programmes may be produced
in-house or with independent production companies. The emergence of the
independent television production sector has led to an increasingly significant
amount of programming being farmed out to these companies, either in their
entirety or as joint productions. This is due to a combination of factors such
as RTE's mandatory obligation to promote the independent production
sector, and the fact that many of their resources, such as producers, directors,
et cetera, are tied up with in-house productions.

It is impossible easily to state which programmes will be produced by RTE or the independent sector. Some quiz shows are produced by RTE, some are not; others are co-productions. Programmes which are co-productions or are independently produced have the company's name listed in *The RTE Guide* and at the end of the programme itself. This information is useful if you want to contribute to an existing programme and wish to know where to write to. You should also bear in mind that an entire series may be 'in the can' before the first show is broadcast – in this case, your suggestions might be considered only for the next series (if any).

As a potential television contributor, you have two options. You may write, first to a production company with your programme idea or take it to RTE yourself. RTE may take to your idea or they may not. The independent production company may like your idea, develop it and approach RTE with it, and get rejected. However, such an approach would in all likelihood be more favourably received than a submission from an unknown. The experienced production company will be in a position to put together a well thought out project proposal. Of course you may approach the independent sector and, if turned down, approach RTE, or vice versa.

A common error with many submissions is that they are very similar to existing programmes. Even if you feel your programme idea is better than an equivalent existing programme (and it may well be), it is unlikely to be developed. RTE will not be inclined to axe an existing programme which seems to be working well, and has built up an audience, in favour of a 'new, improved' version. Writers should also be aware of the considerable time (at least six months) which elapses before a programme gets from script to screen.

Established TV writers tend to keep one eye on RTE and the other on the independent sector. Just because you have been rejected by RTE doesn't mean that you have no other options.

A potential screenwriter should also be aware that there are a number of funding agencies whose function is to develop film and television scripts. A script which has received a substantial amount of finance from the RTE/BBC script fund, for example, stands a better chance of ultimately being produced than a script which has no such aid. The reality is that once you are awarded funding for script development, you receive all sorts of invaluable non-monetary assistance. The script-funding bodies would come in for severe criticism if few of the scripts in which they invested money were produced.

The reality for today's television writer is that you have to know how to produce the script as well as write it.

USEFUL TERMS AND TERMINOLOGY

New writers to the business are often bemused to know that sometimes the film or TV script is actually the last thing that gets written. Production companies, grant-making agencies and broadcasters often ask for the script as the last resort. In the first instance they usually prefer to see treatments, character breakdowns, et cetera. In order to progress to this scriptwriting stage, the writer must be aware of the mechanics and realities of film.

BUDGETS

Budgets play a crucial role in determining whether or not a film is made. You must be aware of the inevitable expenses which accrue when producing a film. You may then write your screenplay bearing such expenses in mind. You will make your producer happier and increase the chances of having your film made if, for example, you write your film with a central Irish location rather than a foreign equivalent.

A typical film budget would have to address many, though not necessarily all, of a myriad categories and sub-categories.

- Location reconnaissance costs which may include: stills/video costs, location costs, subsistence costs, transport/expenses (air-fares/rail/taxi, research costs), telephone/fax bills.

- Cast/casting costs: casting fees, director's fees, video/Polaroid costs, casting venue hire, principal artists fees, semi-featured fees, children's fees, chaperones' fees, extras voice-over fees, stunt persons' fees, transport/hotel costs, electrical costs, gaffer, generator/fuel/mileage allowances, lighting van hire, lighting hire, electricity charges, et cetera.

- Unit salaries: fees for the producer, director, production manager, production assistant, assistant director(s), continuity person, production secretary, lighting camera person, camera operator, focus-puller, clapper/loader, grip, art director, prop buyer/dresser, riggers/stagehands, stills photographer, special-effects person, animal handler, consultants, security staff, et cetera.

- Art costs: set designers' wages, artwork costs, props purchase, props hire, wardrobe costs, wigs hire, mock-ups/labels/sfx costs, model materials, make-up expenses.

- Equipment costs: hire of; camera, lens, filters, video players, geared/fluid heads, legs short/tall, dolly/crane, sound recorder/playback machines, mikes, autocues, camera car, helicopter, etc.

- Location expenses: studio hire, production-office hire, dressing-room hire, canteen charges, security charges, transport charges.

- Construction costs: construction manager's wage, carpenters' wages, painters' wages, plasterers'/plumbers' wages, riggers' wages, construction materials.

- Location costs: location hire, location-office costs, air/rail/taxi fares, mileage allowances, hotel bills, catering charges, telephones/fax charges.

- Film stock costs: negative/reversal processing costs, videotape costs.

- Laboratory costs: developing costs, rush printing costs, optical sound transfer costs, opticals/titles, negative cutting costs, negative cleaning costs, telecine charge, viewing room hire, shipping/couriers charges.

- Sound costs: sound studio hire, music costs (copyright charges and/or musician fees).

- Editing costs: editor fees, cutting-room hire, telecine/grading costs, negative-cleaning costs, tape off-line, tape on-line costs, graphics/paintbox costs, caption-camera costs, intermediate tape costs, copies/cassette costs.

- Sundries: insurance cover, rain cover, carnets, freight expenses, vat depreciation/poe, catering costs, overhead allowances, gratuities, contingency fees, completion guarantees and, of course, the writer's fee.

Naturally most programme submissions would not include all of the above – not every film would require the use of a helicopter, for example. Many of the above expenses (such as wages) may be partially or wholly waived. Some of the above items can also be had at little or no charge. A shot on a beach would not usually require a location hire charge, unless the beach is private.

A writer should be aware of such charges. Quentin Tarantino purposely wrote *Reservoir Dogs* as an inexpensive feature. The main location is a deserted LA warehouse, which was filmed in a deserted LA warehouse; other locations of lesser importance, such as an office, a public toilet and a flat roof, would not need to be specially made. His *Pulp Fiction,* however, was written when he had considerable budgets available to him. One set – the restaurant (for a ten-minute sequence) – was purposely built for the film and was reckoned to have cost upwards of a million dollars.

CHARACTER BREAKDOWN

This refers to the description of the main characters in a film or TV drama. These descriptions are normally placed at the front of a script so that a producer can visualise the characters easily and form a vague opinion of whom might be suitable/available to play the roles. The character breakdown can reveal some potential flaw in the proposed story. If the lead characters are stereotyped or clichéd, the script could be in trouble. A breakdown might look like:

<u>**Characters:**</u>

KAREN: a woman in her thirties. She is a strong-willed executive who feels obliged to over-compensate in the male-dominated boardroom. At the end of the day she goes to a gym and 'kick-boxes' a punch-bag. The instructor can always tell what kind of day she's had by the state of the punch-bag. She is up for a key promotion against a male colleague who hates her guts. She nurses a deep secret – she had to reinvent herself, she got out of a bad marriage and alcoholism and put herself through college. She was economical with the truth on her initial job application. She knows that if her ultimate boss – a staunch Catholic, conservative – finds out, she will not get the promotion.

KEN: Karen's colleague and competitor for the same promotion. He is in his thirties and, while on the surface he is pleasant to Karen, he in fact dislikes her intensely. This is partially because she rejected his advances one night. He suspects that Karen nurses some secret and carefully starts to dig away at her past. He has few scruples and will use any information he can find to blackmail Karen and get whatever he wants. He is quite brilliant and got where he is by the use of a first-rate mind. His genius has led to arrogance which is increasingly divorcing him from reality. What began as a careful study of Karen starts to become a compulsion. He steadily becomes obsessed by her and stalks her; he monitors her calls. When he fails to get the promotion, something snaps. He has never failed to get anything in his life. His secret obsession is leading him on a personal path of violence.

Character breakdowns of minor characters reflect their importance in the story. A character who makes a brief appearance in a script might earn a two– or three-word description – Two policewomen; Weedy construction workers; Waiter in his thirties; Teenage boy are all acceptable descriptions.

CUTAWAYS

A scene can have considerably enhanced dramatic potential when contrasted with another scene. In essence, you can either DISSOLVE from one scene to another or CUT from one to the other. You might write DISSOLVE when you want the end of one scene to overlap with the beginning of another. Dissolves are useful if you wish to suggest the passage of time or create a relaxed, easy-going atmosphere. You might also use it if you wish to burn a particular image in to the audience's mind.

```
(1)   EXTERIOR. A WORLD WAR ONE FOX HOLE.

      Nearby shellfire. Bullets ricochet overhead.

      A dying soldier, pushes, with effort, a letter into

      his empty water bottle. He seals it and slumps down.


      The bottle slips from his fingers on to the ground.

      A nearby explosion tosses dirt into the hole,

      covering up the bottle apart from its cap.


      A medic arrives, his boot presses the bottle further

      into the ground. The medic leaves, with the dead

      soldier.


      A piece of mud marks the bottle's resting place.


      DISSOLVE TO
```

Cutaways and cutting are vital components in the writer's toolkit. Frequent switching between scenes adds pace to a film, and is especially used when heightened tension or action is required. For example:

(1)   INTERIOR. CAR. DAY.

JACKIE is driving quickly down the road, her foot pressed hard against the accelerator. Cars beep their horns as she dashes through a red light. She reaches into a purse as she drives and pulls out a pair of tights. She grips it between her teeth and hacks at it with a nail file. She severs one leg and pulls it down over her head as a mask. She reaches into the glove box and pulls out a revolver. She screeches to a halt outside a bank. She brakes so suddenly that the pistol goes off - squirting water on to the windscreen.

CUT TO

(2)   INTERIOR. BANK. DAY.

BRIAN the porter checks his watch - it is almost closing time. He approaches the main door, keys jangle in his hand. He glances around and purposely decreases his pace across the room.

The CUTAWAY SHOT differs from the CUT TO direction in that the jump to another scene is momentary, and the main scene is frequently returned to. Here is a complete shot without any cutting:

```
JOHN walks slowly across the room. He grips the door
handle, opens the door and suddenly is hit hard over
the head by a masked intruder.
```

Here is the same scene with the introduction of the CUTAWAY device.

```
JOHN walks slowly across the room.


CUTAWAY TO HALLWAY
Masked intruder waits outside door.
John grips the door handle, opens the door and is
hit hard over the head.
```

While the first passage is eventful, and surprises an audience – a sometimes desirable effect – the latter passage, by contrast, has no surprise but is considerably more suspenseful. We know that there is an intruder waiting to strike; we wonder if John will open the door or not. Will the phone ring in time to warn him? The CUTAWAY – sometimes abbreviated to C/A – is a useful drama-heightening device, increasing simultaneous action and compressing time. In the first passage, we saw John walk the full several yards across the floor. In the second version, we see him begin his walk but we don't actually see John making the walk. We take it for granted. A potentially dull, needless segment has thus been surgically removed.

We can add even more suspense through piling on the cutaways:

```
John walks slowly across the room.


C/A TO HALLWAY

Masked intruder waits by door.


CUT BACK TO ROOM

John's hand, pausing on handle.


C/A TO HALLWAY

Intruder's hand tightens on hammer.


CUT BACK TO ROOM

John turns the handle and opens the door slightly.


C/A TO HALLWAY

Intruder raises arm to strike.


CUT BACK TO ROOM

John pauses, he remembers he's forgotten something,

he closes door and hurries back to office.
```

Phew. The build-up of different shots can thus be used in a highly dramatic fashion. Note that nothing very dramatic actually happens; it is the juxtaposition of shots which cause the tension.

Remember, however, that as a writer your primary duty is to come up with darn good stories, and you should not worry untowardly about camera angles or scene numbers. An awareness of the medium's advantages and limitations should be apparent in your script. Wesley Burrowes advises writers:

> not to worry about the technical details or how you express the thing, or about close-ups, medium close-ups and tilts and all of the technical expressions. These are not a worry to us at all. We just want to see what way people's imaginations work and how far they understand the characters. The trick is to write down what you see coming out of the TV screen, what you want to see coming out. How it gets to that stage is a matter for the technicians inside, and in fact, sometimes when you give over elaborate TV directions and so on, you're just succeeding in annoying the director, because he is saying, 'Who the hell does this guy think he is? I'm the director here.'

PRODUCTION PLAN (SCHEDULE)

This is a document which is sometimes required by production funding agencies. It is highly specialised and writers are not expected to be able to fill it in. This is where your independent production company becomes essential. Independent production companies should be able to draw up a production plan (sometimes known as the production schedule). This document contains the proposed plan for a film's production. It may include the exact number of days a film is to be shot and how much it would cost. It would also take into account the preparation for the shoot and the post-production required.

SYNOPSIS

A synopsis is the screenplay's story encapsulated in about three or four sentences. A synopsis should capture the essence of the story. It is usually a good idea to present a synopsis using crisp, clear images. Avoid going into the psychological meaning or philosophical sub-texts. This is how the synopsis for one film might have read:

> `Jurassic Park` is set in the late 20th century when man has discovered how to reconstitute extinct animals using DNA taken from amber-preserved mosquitoes. A wealthy biologist plans to open a theme park on a tropical island where living dinosaurs are the attraction. Things start to go horribly wrong for the first visitors, however, when the dinosaurs escape from their pens and become uncontrollable.

SCENES

A scene consists of a number of shots which together complete a defined film segment. When you are writing a scene you need to include essential information for the director/producer. It should be clear from your script where the scene takes place, who is in the scene, what's happening, and if it is day or night. Scenes are numbered consecutively.

A *master scene* is one which is comprised of a complete, self-contained film passage. It may contain a number of small sub-scenes.

SHOTS

A shot refers to what the camera records. A shot of a house is thus an uninterrupted recording of a house, a shot of a street is the recording of a street. A scene (a self-contained film sequence) normally contains a number of shots.

Shots are normally divided into several categories, each of them serving different functions. All of them are used to convey different information.

The *establishing shot* informs the viewer where the action is taking place. An establishing shot might be of a building, a speeding car, an aircraft, a prairie, et cetera. Then once the scene is established, the subsequent shot will normally be in that building, car or aircraft, or on that prairie.

The *long shot* is when the main focus of attention is some distance away. A long shot might therefore be of a car – a speck in the distance racing across a desert, plumes of dust rising up behind it. The long shot is in this case also doubles as an *establishing shot.* The long shot is useful because it puts the subject in perspective. Using long shots we can see that a traffic jam extends for miles, that every window in a house is broken. A long shot can be fifty metres from the subject or fifty light years.

In the *mid shot,* the background becomes less important and the subject is far closer. We can see definition now – the colour and make of the car is clear, the person driving is now seen to be young, male and wearing a baseball cap.

In the *close-up,* the subject of the shot fills the whole frame. We can see the colour of the driver's eyes.

Sometimes these shots are qualified by the adjective *extreme;* in this case EXTREME CLOSE-UP means that a person's eye, perhaps, might fill the whole frame.

It is important when scriptwriting that the scene is set before further information is passed on. A film opening with a close-up of a man's eye makes no sense unless it placed in context. This close-up is confusing – which, if not the desired effect, is inappropriate. A film might therefore begin as follows:

FADE UP

(1)   **EXT. DESERT. DAY.**

CREDITS ROLL

A desert plain. The sun beats down. What looks like smoke rises in the distance.

We are closer now and see that the smoke is actually sand thrown up from a speeding car

We are closer still. The car is yellow, with what looks like a jet strapped to the back – it is obviously purposely built for speed.

The car rapidly approaches at great speed, filling the screen. Suddenly it is on us – and seems about to run us down. At the last second everything freezes. The helmet of the driver fills the whole screen in an EXTREME CLOSE-UP.

END CREDITS

TREATMENTS

A treatment could be described as a detailed plot. It normally contains a scene-by-scene breakdown of the proposed film. It can therefore be quite substantial in length.

A treatment normally indicates where the scene takes place, who's in the scene, and what the action is. A treatment excerpt may look very similar to the film script, details such as scene numbers, shots, dialogue though don't tend to be included:

```
EXT. NIGHT

It is a dark and icy cold winter's night in a barren
part of the countryside. Sleet rattles down. There
are no lights to be seen and no one would willingly
venture out on a night such as this.


Suddenly headlights pierce the gloom.


INT. CAR. NIGHT

A car drives down a lonely country road. The driver
is in silhouette. We cannot tell if the driver is
male or female. The driver strains to see through
the windscreen.
```

EXT. CAR

The driver pulls up beside a signpost which is
bathed in the headlight's beams. A map is unfolded
on the driver's lap. The driver peers through the
windscreen at the signpost which is half-obscured by
some trees. The driver turns off the engine,
unfastens the safety belt, unlocks the door and
steps out of the car. The driver moves to the
signpost and examines it, comparing the directions
to the map. The driver is illuminated by the beams
and we can see that the driver is a woman, KAREN, in
her thirties, wearing jeans and a thick sweater. She
is obviously frustrated; the map and the signpost
don't seem to correlate at all. She swears and heads
back to the car. She hops in.

INT. CAR

Karen places the map on the passenger seat, puts on
her seat belt, locks the car door out of habit and
then reaches for the keys in the ignition. The keys
are no longer there. Karen's face shows surprise.
She glances in the mirror. There is the silhouette
of someone who wasn't there before.

VISUAL STYLE

This is usually the director's vision of the script and takes the form of a description of how the manuscript is to be best filmed.

This four- or five-sentence description might say that a particular colour is to dominate each scene (an example might be Greenaway's *The Cook, the Thief, His Wife and Her Lover* where sumptuous red dominated the dining room). You might say that there will be considerable use of light and shadows (as there was in Alan Parker's *Angel Heart* where Robert De Niro's Devil character almost literally emerges from the shadows, or Orson Welles's *A Touch of Evil*, where there is an uninterrupted eleven-minute opening shot. If the film is to use flashbacks from the present to, say, 50 years ago, the director might use colour film for the present segments of the film and black and white for the portions set in the past. The Steven Spielberg-directed film *Schindler's List* (based on the true story of a World War II concentration camp) used such a technique. He said that he chose to shoot the majority of the film in black and white because his only vision of the war was based on the newsreel images of that time. The director of *Dick Tracy*, starring Warren Beatty, Madonna and Al Pacino, obviously decided to go for a look that would suggest the film's comic-book origins. The only colours used for the sets, cars and costumes were the bright, primary colours typical of an American comic book.

Now while the style is ultimately the director's decision, you can influence it by the way you write the script. If you would like a particular colour to dominate a scene, then you should emphasise those colours in your script. If you believe that a black and white grainy film would work best, you could mention this in the film's synopsis.

W R I T I N G   F I L M

Essentially there are two types of film script: the writer's script, which contains all of the dialogue and the scene descriptions; and the shooting or master script, which contains all of the same information plus further details required by the editor, director and technicians. While it is neither necessary nor desirable to clutter up your script with technical directions it is important to understand their function. (The director will probably ignore most of them and have his or her own directions pencilled in anyway). This way you can use the minimum amount of technical directions coupled with language couched in such a way that the director will do what you want anyway.

There are some commonly used 'filmspeak' terms which you may decide to use on your script.

- Action: what the camera records.

- Camera angle – often *low angle* or *high angle*: the position of camera relative to the subject. A low-angle shot of a person means the camera is low down, looking up at the person.

- Pan: a gentle sweeping camera movement often expressed as *Camera pans left* or similar. *Tilt* is identical to pan except that the camera moves in a vertical motion.

- Point of view (POV) – usually written as *Harry's POV* or *Harry's point of view*: the camera records the action as seen though Harry's eyes.

- Shot: an uninterrupted film sequence. *Two-shot (2S)* means that there are two people in the frame. *Dolly-shot* refers to a shot taken from a camera mounted on a dolly – a wheeled platform.

- VO: voice-over. We hear but do not see someone speak.

The first item on the script is FADE IN or FADE UP (note capitals). These are interchangeable terms. The next item is the scene number. The number of the scene depends on where it is in the script – very simply Scene 5 directly follows Scene 4. You must then indicate where the scene is taking place, if the scene is indoors or out, and if it's taking place at night or by day. An example of a film opening might be:

```
FADE UP

12.   INT. MODERN KITCHEN. DAY.

      HARRY - a man aged about 40 - is sitting at a table

      eating cornflakes. He is wearing boxer shorts and a

      faded T-shirt. He looks up at a wall clock.
```

Another example would be:

```
FADE UP

15.   EXT. OCEAN. NIGHT.

      HARRY walks along a deserted strand. He looks

      around, reaches into a pocket and produces a

      flashlight. He switches the light on and off

      quickly. A light from far out to sea responds.
```

Sometimes you may include the shot numbers, though this isn't usually necessary until someone expresses an interest in seeing a further draft of the script. Shot numbers are listed in alphabetical or numerical order – this is often a case of personal preferences. The same scenes could be expressed as:

```
        FADE UP

12.     INT. MODERN KITCHEN. DAY.

        (a) HARRY - a man aged about 40 - is sitting at a
        table eating cornflakes. He is wearing boxer shorts
        and a faded T-shirt.

        (b) He looks up at a wall clock.
```

or

```
        FADE UP

15.     EXT. OCEAN. NIGHT.

        (1) LARRY walks along a deserted strand.

        (2) He looks around, reaches into a pocket and
        produces a flashlight.

        (3) He switches the light on and off quickly.

        (4) A light from far out to sea responds.
```

Points to note: directions (i.e. FADE UP, CUT TO, et cetera) and scene settings (i.e. EXT. OCEAN. NIGHT) are normally written in upper-case lettering.

You may choose to underline these directions and/or type them out in bold lettering. This depends on the tools and the amount of time you have at your disposal.

Scene descriptions are generally written from margin to margin.

A character is usually expressed in upper-case lettering the first time he or she is introduced in a scene. Thereafter, whenever the character is referred to in the stage directions or scene description, normal lower-case lettering will be used. Whenever a character speaks, their name is expressed in upper-case lettering in the centre of the page. What they have to say is written in a narrow column underneath. This column is sited well away from the margins on either side of the page.

Sound directions and voice-overs follow a similar format to that used for the dialogue. A fuller sample of a film script might be:

```
FADE UP
```

(1)   EXT. BOG-LAND. SUMMER'S DAY.

```
                    MUSIC
```

```
A curlew swirls in the air after insects. A tractor

can be heard in the distance. We see a man cutting

turf in the distance. We move closer; there is a

young boy in shorts on the bank beside him.
```

```
                    JOE (V.O.)

          I suppose as summers go, that

          one was no different from any

          other, but that's not how I

          remember it.
```

SPECIMEN FILM SCRIPT

1

FADE UP

1.   **A MOUNTAINOUS AREA. DAY.**

CREDITS ROLL

A wild land covered in woods and hills. Birds fly through the air. Deer can be seen nibbling on the edge of some woods. Rabbits tumble in a clearing. Icy water gushes over a cliff down to a waterfall hundreds of feet below. This seems like a tranquil land and time. All is harmony.

END CREDITS

We continue on our leisurely exploration of this land. Suddenly, we see a plume of dark smoke rising from behind a hill.

We move closer and follow the plume down to its source. We see a scene of brutal mayhem. Smoke rises from a burning village. Tunic-clad bodies lie everywhere. Here and there pockets of resistance are being brutally put down by sword-wielding raiders.

2

A short distance from the village stretches a grassy field. The tall blades stir as someone stealthily sneaks away from the carnage.

Four of the raiders - all young males wearing the bright tunics and cloaks of young warriors - are congratulating themselves on the success of the raid. They playfully punch each other.

TADHG, the youngest is about sixteen and is a reluctant warrior. He's more at home minding pigs.

CORMAC, the leader, is the most vicious of the four. He is easily angered and can become violent.

CONGAL is the brother of CORMAC. He is a simpleton who has a permanent smile fixed to his face.

The last man is nicknamed RUADH on account of his red beard. He is probably the most intelligent of the men. He could be the leader, only he can't be bothered.

3

One of them notices the grass bending in the field. They grin at the prospect of fresh sport. They quietly sneak up on the spot where the escapee lies. They each have, poised at the ready, long throwing spears which bend under their own weight.

They surround the spot where the victim lies hidden.

As one they charge forward and plunge their spears into empty earth.

At that moment an indistinct figure surfaces some distance behind them, and, limping, flees the field.

The warriors are puzzled for a moment at encountering nothing. They spy the retreating figure and are delighted: the fun is not yet over. They yell out in exuberance and pound each other's shields. Then, all the while making yapping sounds like dogs, they bound off across the field after the figure who diminishes in the distance.

4

CUT TO

2. **EXTERIOR. NARROW RIVER ALLEY. STEEP HILLS DROP DOWN
    TOWARDS VALLEY FLOOR. DAY.**

DOWNBEAT IRISH MUSIC - BODHRÁN

A wild, rugged, exposed wilderness.

MUSIC ABRUPTLY UP SEVERAL TEMPOS

- BODHRÁN BEATS URGENTLY

Suddenly a girl's face is seen up close as she falls
headlong forward. She has just crossed the stream on
the floor of the valley and is about to climb the
hill on the other side. She is close to exhaustion.
She is visible for only a few moments. Her name is
SCATHACH. She is about thirteen. She conveys a sense
of absolute urgency. Her matted hair, torn cloak and
filthy face all suggest that she has been running
through brambles and dirty bog for some time. It is
quite evident that she is fleeing for her life.

5

She stoops and tightens a strip of cloth around her side. She gasps in agony. Blood can be seen seeping through the cloth. She has obviously been wounded during the raid on the village.

She glances behind her and scrambles on up the steep incline towards the relative safety of some woods at the top.

Four pairs of legs hurdle a tree trunk easily and race on downhill towards the stream at the bottom of valley ...

SCATHACH approaches the top of hill. She is halfway up a steep incline. Behind her the four men hop and skip down the hill towards the valley floor. Soon they will be following her up the hill she now desperately climbs.

The four men, whooping and shrieking at the chase, are closing the distance rapidly. They pause where SCATHACH rested after dashing through the stream.

6

CORMAC bends down and rubs a finger in the droplets of blood on the grass. All grin. They sense the end is near for their quarry. CORMAC puts his finger in his mouth, tasting blood.

SCATHACH is nearer to the top of the hill now. The edge of the woods at the top seem within reach.

The pursuers have crossed the narrow valley floor. They begin to climb up the hill a short distance behind SCATHACH.

SCATHACH is almost at the top. The hunters appear in the background. They are gaining fast.

SCATHACH runs into a small grove of trees. A branch snags a string round her shoulders. This, plus her weakened condition due to the pursuit and loss of blood, cause her to collapse. She can go no further. She must rest to gather her breath. She reaches for the string, which turns out to be part of a sling-shot. To her chagrin she discovers it has broken.

7

The men are halfway up the hill now and jubilant at the prospect of catching their prey.

SCATHACH has finished retying her sling-shot. She reaches into a pocket for ammunition but discovers she has nothing. Desperately she runs her fingers through the grass, searching for a stone. She finds some and discards them as unsuitable. After what seems like an eternity she finds one of suitable weight and size.

The four men come to an abrupt full stop, momentarily surprised as their quarry has stopped running. Their grins at the prospect of an easy catch and of the carnal rewards vanish as they see SCATHACH.

She stands up poised to strike.

The men calculate the distance between them and break into sudden loud guffaws.

8

SCATHACH

(<u>Shouts</u>) Step no further or
there will be one less of you.
My village burns, my people
butchered. Haven't you done
enough?

The four men laugh.

CORMAC

(<u>Shouts</u>) No!

RUADH, laughing helplessly, points up the hill.

RUADH

She has as much chance of
hitting us as Tadhg here has of
growing whiskers ...

SCATHACH, with a determined look, spins the sling-
shot round and round. It whirls so fast that the air
whistles through it. She releases the stone.

TV & FILM WRITING

9

Empty landscape. The four raiders appear to have disappeared. There is no sign of them.

Suddenly three of them stand up, brushing themselves off. They obviously have dived for cover. They chuckle at their foolishness. The very idea of a man ducking to avoid a woman ... Suddenly they are aware of a gap in their ranks. Their expressions change. They glance down.

CONGAL lies flat out. His feet point up the hill.

The three men look down at their fallen comrade and look up the hill. They dive to the ground.

The three men lie down, facing up the hill. CONGAL faces down.. A pair of feet interrupts the line of heads which stare anxiously up towards SCATHACH.

TADHG

You think she's out?

10

RUADH

This is Ireland, lad. Stones
are one thing she'll not be
short of.

CORMAC

I don't know. Tadhg, stand up
there like a good lad and see.

TADHG, the youngest, is scared stiff.

TADHG

But, but if she does and I do,
I, I, I'll be killed.

RUADH

Then we'll know, won't we?

RUADH and TADHG look ahead tactfully as CORMAC
crawls down to CONGAL's head. He lifts it tenderly.
A trickle of blood rolls out of CONGAL's mouth.

11

CORMAC

(<u>Low, menacing – the pursuit is</u>
<u>no longer a game</u>) I'll have
you, badb [crow/war goddess].
If not this day, then the next,
by Lugh and all the gods.
I swear it.

CORMAC stands up, unafraid of any impending
missiles.
TADHG stands up warily.
RUADH surreptitiously picks up CONGAL'S discarded
axe – it is better than his own. He stands up.
CORMAC faces up the hill and slips out of his tunic.
The others do likewise. Soon all they wear is
something akin to a loincloth. Each, though, wears a
torque around his neck.

SCATHACH has vanished.

The men, carrying their weapons, begin an easy lope
up the hill.

12

DISSOLVE TO

3   **EXTERIOR. WOODS, SOMETIME LATER. EVENING.**

SCATHACH squats beside a stream. Carefully and tenderly she bathes her wound. She winces as she does so. She gets up eventually and moves on, picking her way slowly around brambles, under overhanging branches, et cetera. She moves slowly, not because she is afraid of her pursuers – she has long since lost them – but due to her weakened condition. She staggers, almost falling, continues on. She lifts her head. She smells something in the distance. She makes a decision and heads in the direction of the scent.

DISSOLVE TO

4   **A CLEARING IN THE WOODS BESIDE LAKE SHORE.**

There is, as seen from Scathach's POV – and half-obscured by trees – a tiny, seasonal camp. A tiny hut has been thrown together. Some turf and sticks lie outside. A goat is tied to a tree by a long halter.

13

An elderly man, MAEL, wears the distinct robes of a file [poet]. He is squatting in front of a small fire, staring into the flames. A fish grills on a spit.

SCATHACH quietly approaches the clearing. She looks over a fallen tree trunk and spies on the man. She winces and drops to her knees. When the spasm passes she looks again towards the fire.

The old man, however, has vanished.

A puzzled SCATHACH gazes drunkenly at the welcome light of the fire. She is very weak and close to collapsing.

She does not notice the sharp point of a sword which ever so slowly edges down towards her face. She is oblivious to the blade which lingers for a moment just beside her cheek. It moves lower, stealthily, towards her neck. After what seems like an age, it is gently pressed against her skin.

14

SCATHACH's eyes open wide.

MAEL

What have we here? (<u>Raises</u>) A
pretty catch indeed. (<u>Lowers
his sword, smiles</u>) Just in time
for supper, too.

SCATHACH

You would not have caught me if
I was well.

MAEL

(<u>Grins</u>) Ah, child. You make
more noise than the wild boars
of the forest. I heard you long
since. (<u>Notices SCATHACH's
wound</u>) You are sick?

SCATHACH

(<u>Smiles weakly</u>) I have felt
better.

W R I T I N G T V D R A M A

There are two types of television drama: the TV film and everything else. The essential difference between a TV film and a cinematic film is that the TV film generally has a significantly lesser budget. TV drama includes writing dramatic reconstructions for documentaries, soap-writing, serial-writing, short dramas and made-for-TV feature-length films.

In film, mood and location is established by the use of interesting and sometimes intrusive camerawork. A film might open with a long, long panning shot of a prairie before anything of significance happens. The action might be seen from, say, a fly's point of view, and so the camera jerks around simulating this. TV writing is very different. TV programmes are written to be shot quickly. A film writer might indicate a character's nervousness by writing several sentences describing a bead of sweat which appears on the character's forehead and rolls down his nose. The director might take the hint and tell the camera operator to zoom in on the bead so that it fills the entire screen. This kind of shot could take all day to film – there's the lighting to set up, the correct lens to be fitted, a make-up person applying glycerine to simulate sweat, the director moaning that the sweat has the wrong texture and insists on another take. A TV writer would create a similar effect by giving the actor a stage direction, such as WIPES FOREHEAD. TV dramas tend to highlight characters and minimise elaborate camerawork.

A TV writer has to write scripts which can be shot quickly with the minimum of fuss. Special effects, moody lighting, helicopter shots can all look marvellous – but they simply are too expensive and take too long to set up. As a TV writer, you must establish mood, tension, et cetera with the one element over which you have some control – the characters. You must get the story across through the actions and the dialogue of the characters.

TV writers are aware that the medium they write for does not have the vast resources a film-writer can call on. The RTE serial *Glenroe* costs about £50,000 per half-hour episode to make. A cinematic film might be three times the running length but may have ten times the budget, if not more. A film could take six months to make; a soap, six days. This time restriction means that the script must be lend itself to economical shooting. If you are writing a short drama, you must fully utilise your sets: one scene might take place inside a shop, the next takes place right outside, the next down the street. A TV producer wouldn't welcome a script which required one 30-second scene set in Donegal and another in Kerry. 'Why can't they both be shot in the same county?, he or she would say, though not perhaps as politely.

TV, like film, is not usually recorded in chronological order. You might write a script containing three separate scenes set in a pub. Those three scenes would be recorded altogether and spliced into the appropriate position in the film in the editing suite. There is a tradition whereby TV directors try not to be intrusive. They do not tend to zoom in on character's faces for extreme tight close-ups or use very low or high angles to shoot scenes. You should write your script so that such references are included only if essential.

TV drama writing tends to be dominated by writers who learned their craft by play-writing. Few TV drama writers have never written plays. Playwrights tend to be good with dialogue and are used to the limitations of imposed by the stage, which are similar to the limitations of TV. A stage playwright has to contain all the action, with a limited number of characters within a finite number of sets – just as a TV writer does.

The general rule of thumb is that as a potential TV writer, you have to be able to demonstrate that you possess a good visual flair with an ability to write good dialogue, all combined with an awareness of the restrictions of the medium.

TV SCRIPTS

Television scripts tend to have a different layout to film scripts. They are in a two column format. The left-hand column is used for vision – what is seen, the second column is used for audio – what is heard.

The two-column format (or a variation of the same) is primarily used for documentaries and some TV dramas, especially soaps. The format tends to have a very dry, workman-like feel to it – descriptions are terse, directions matter-of-fact.

TV dramas which are written with lots of unusual and artistic shots in mind are normally written like film scripts.

SPECIMEN TV SCRIPT

Fireside Tales

A series of 28 min. dramas for children

Episode 1/6

FADE UP

1.   EXT. DAY. SUMMER.

EST. SHOT

SCOUT/GIRL GUIDE

'JAMBOREE'.

TINNY 'POP' MUSIC PLAYED

FROM P.A. SYSTEM.

1

CREDITS ROLL

C/U A YOUNG,

UNIFORMED GIRL GUIDE

CLUTCHING A PLATE OF

FOOD.

WE FOLLOW HER AS SHE

WEAVES HER WAY AMONG

A MYRIAD GUY ROPES,

THROUGH CAMP.

END CREDITS	**SCOUTMASTER**
	<u>(Voice Over)</u>
C/A SEVERAL YOUNG	It must have seemed
BOYS ATTEMPTING TO	peaceful, living the life
PUT UP A TENT;	of a hermit in woods such
	as these.
C/A GUIDES PLAY HIDE	However, once you emerged
AND SEEK IN TREES;	from the forest depths,
	you had to tread with
C/A SCOUTS UNPACK	great care. For this was
RUCKSACKS	

2

L/S GUIDE POV

GUIDE HEADS TOWARDS A

LARGE GROUP WHO SIT

AROUND A HUGE,

BLAZING CAMPFIRE

LISTENING INTENTLY TO

ELDERLY GENTLEMAN –

THE SCOUTMASTER.

C/A TO

A SCOUT PLAYFULLY
CUFFS ANOTHER WITH A
FLAT HAND AS IF IT
WERE AN AXE. THE
'VICTIM' DIES IN MOCK
AGONY.

once an unsafe and savage
land. Only the Druids or
the File – the poets –
could pass without fear
of an outlaw's axe.

C/A

A GIRL GUIDE WHISPERS
INTO ANOTHER'S EAR AT
THIS. BOTH BURST OUT
LAUGHING.

Sometimes, the need grew
for cattle, slaves or
even women

3

C/U SCOUTMASTER WHO
STIRS THE FIRE
ABSENTMINDEDLY WITH
HIS STICK. WE FOLLOW
FLYING SPARKS AND
SLOWLY TILT UP,
FOLLOWING PLUME OF
SMOKE

DISSOLVE TO OUT-OF-
FOCUS SMOKE

SMOKE CLEARS, FOLLOW
PLUME DOWN. THE
SMOKE COMES NOT FROM
A CAMPFIRE BUT A
BURNING HUT

When this happened, the men
AND women - for women were
treated more or less as
equals then ventured forth
joined in the battles, woe
betide any village or
villagers who stood in the
raiders' way.

THERE IS A FAINT SOUND WHICH
GROWS STEADILY LOUDER. IT IS
THE SOUND OF A VILLAGE BEING
RAVAGED. MEN/WOMEN
SHOUT/SCREAM, SOUNDS OF
SWORD ON SWORD

There was once such a
village on this spot, you'd
never know it now. A
thriving village until one
dark day
SCOUTMASTER'S VOICE FADES

4

W R I T I N G   S O A P S

Long-running television series became known as 'soaps' in the United States because washing-detergent manufacturers were the main sponsors of cheap, daytime melodramas aimed at housewives. American night-time shows are often glamorous, with settings dominated by wealth and power, and are epitomised by *Dallas* and *Dynasty*. British soaps, however, tend towards depicting characters in ordinary settings. UK soaps (on which Irish soaps are modelled) feature ordinary characters who are not all that removed from the viewers themselves. Your average viewer probably has had a drink in a pub not all that different from the Rover's in *Coronation Street*, and is likely, at some point, to walk down through an outdoor market similar to the one in *EastEnders*. There is also a more subtle distinction between UK and US soaps. Mary Halpin, former senior storyline writer of *Fair City*, points out that:

> US soaps are very patriarchal, in the sense that they have very strong male characters. UK soaps tend to be matriarchal; in other words, they are led by strong women. If you take a character like Bet Lynch in *Coronation Street*, she is very clearly a matriarchal figure and acts a kind of substitute mother to the likes of Raquel. The character of Hanna in *Fair City* is similarly powerful. I think that it may be the case in America that men are perceived as being stronger. The men in the British and Irish soaps tend to be rather weak in general. They may be bad, some of them, but they are weak and bad, like our Bela, who is counterbalanced by the character of Harry Molloy who is a good husband and father. Bela is a very striking character and audiences can identify with him because there are plenty of Belas walking around the streets in Dublin. Essentially he is a weak man.

Soaps represent a challenging medium for a writer. Soap-writers have to provide dialogue for characters which they did not create and build a story line towards a climax they may not write. Soap-writers tend to write a block of episodes, all of which have to link seamlessly into what other writers have written. They have to set up stories that will be continued by other writers, and to complete stories provided by previous writers. Each half-hour episode usually has three stories contained in it: there is a story line which lasts over many weeks, a shorter story line which is resolved in a few weeks, and a comic story line which is often set up and resolved within the episode itself. *Glenroe* script editor, Sean McCarthy, comments:

> It's a difficult discipline. I mean you have to write it at 26 minutes long, no shorter than that; it has to be filmed in a pair, with another episode – two days in the studio, two days in outside broadcast, and open day with a lightweight, single camera unit. It has to have about fifteen scenes in it, balanced between interiors and exteriors; it has to have about fourteen and a half characters. You then have to work to other people's story lines, you have to write for characters that you have not invented yourself, and be able to do that accurately. They are characters who are extremely well known; they are characters that are better known than your next-door neighbour is to you. They're national figures, and people will instinctively know if they're right or wrong. It is not always easy to get into the skin of these characters and write automatically for them.

A script editor will be better able to make an informed decision about a writer if they receive a sample television script. (You really are wasting your time sending off extracts from your novel-in-progress.) You'll have a far better chance if you submit sample television scenes which closely resemble the soap's style.

We don't ask for submissions of scripts or story lines for *Glenroe* at all; we do not encourage that. We don't particularly like getting them and they're not of any great use to us. What I like to see is a sample of a writer's work, usually written for the screen, not too far from the world of *Glenroe*. In other words, it should have a sense of humour, it should be about Ireland in the twentieth century, and it should be manageable from my point of view. In other words, submitting a 110,000-word novel is not going to be a great deal of help to me, it would just take me longer to read the thing then to read a good sharp sample of somebody's work. If then there is some kind of nearness to what *Glenroe* is about, then I would talk to that writer. I'd look for other samples of that writer's work. If that writer showed some promise, I would then probably ask him or her to write a sample scene, or a sample half-episode, or even a sample episode, and, depending how well the writer did with that, we might take it further.

Sean McCarthy, Glenroe *Script Editor*

WRITING FOR *FAIR CITY*

Fair City is set in a fictitious, Dublin inner-city area. Its characters are mainly working class people who, if employed, work as hairdressers, barmen, or pizza-makers. The series has been running for four years. Initially it received a roasting from both critics and the public alike, but with the employment of newer Irish writers and an emphasis on better scripts, the series now maintains a respectable audience and does not lag far behind the established *Glenroe* in the audience ratings. *Fair City* is a half-hour programme and goes out twice a week with an omnibus edition on Sundays. The programme is broadcast during the autumn and spring television season and breaks for the summer.

Writing for any soap is a collaborative effort. *Fair City* is no exception. There are several layers of personnel who have an input to what each character says and does on the screen. There is a story line team responsible for mapping out what happens to each of the characters over the forthcoming year. These events or stories are then divided up among the number of episodes in the series. A dialogue writer then takes each of these stories and puts the dialogue to them. When each episode is completed it is sent to the script editor, who ensures that the script is the correct running length for shooting.

WRITING FOR *GLENROE*

Glenroe is an Irish rural drama set in the eponymous, fictitious Wicklow village. It was originally written entirely by veteran writer Wesley Burrowes, who, apart from numerous stage plays, wrote the *Glenroe* precursor, the rural-based *Bracken* – starring Gabriel Byrne. Wesley has now cut back on his work load, choosing to write about half the series, thus allowing other opportunities for writers.

Glenroe is written in 36 weekly episodes of 26 minutes each. It is broadcast at the prime 8.30 p.m. viewing slot on Sunday nights.

Most of the people who work on *Glenroe* usually have some considerable theatrical background. Writers tend to have written many stage plays; the actors have appeared in numerous stage productions; and many of the series directors have stage directing experience also.

The key person working on *Glenroe*, from the writer's point of view, is the script editor, Sean McCarthy, who started professional life as an actor. He moved to Edinburgh where he began writing stage plays. Later he was asked to write for BBC television, which he did before moving to the Abbey Theatre where he ran the script department, working on the development of a number of new writers such as Bernard Farrell, Neil Donnelly and Frank McGuinness.

The script editor's role on *Glenroe* involves liaising with the various writers involved in the show, ensuring that they send in their material on time, suggesting changes to submitted material and finally editing down the scripts to broadcast length. Sean McCarthy describes a fairly typical day:

> I received a script from Wesley this morning, of Episode 24. I will read that this afternoon, make some notes on it, talk to Wesley about it. Then the story associate will read it and she will look at it in much more practical terms. If there are any changes necessary – obviously, with Wesley's scripts, there usually aren't a lot of changes necessary – I have to check it against the story lines that are gone before and the story lines that are to come. I then get that episode out to Harriet O'Carroll, who's writing the next two episodes. I've already had a breakdown of her episodes in on Friday, I asked her to re-adjust a whole lot of those, she'll be faxing the re-adjusted one of those at the end of today. I'll need then to have a discussion with her, and with Maeve Ingoldsby, about where they're taking the next story lines which always get altered slightly, even though we've written them down and agreed them, you know, and we allow that. It's much more flexible than *Fair City*. It can be, because *Fair City* goes out twice a week.

SPECIMEN *GLENROE* SCRIPT

TV scripts are written to be shot quickly and efficiently. They are noted for the paucity of camera directions and special effects. For this reason they don't have the complex layout of a film script. They tend to be a simple two-column layout. Dialogue and the actors' action is in the right-hand column, while the left-hand column is left blank. The director will later pencil his or her camera directions into this space.

From Opening Sequence

/

BIDDY AND MILEY WALK DOWN
FROM THE BUNGALOW ACROSS THE
GRASS. DOWN THE STEPS AND
OVER TO DINNY'S HOUSE. THEY
TALK AS THEY WALK.

MILEY
Will YOU start or will I?

BIDDY
I'd say HE'LL start.

MILEY
You think he'll still be
vexed?

BIDDY
I wouldn't say vexed. Berserk
maybe.

MILEY

Well if that's the case,
we'll just stand there
quietly, let him roar and
shout all he wants, and when
he's finished, we'll tell him
calmly that we're sorry for
all that happened and that it
won't happen again./

BIDDY

Grovel./

MILEY

(NODS) But in a dignified
way.

THEY CLIMB OVER STILE/

To *2S Dinny\Teasy

To 9 Sc. 2 Int. Dinny's
Kitchen

áá
Episode 9/ 1 ˚Loc: EXT. BYRNES YARD/COTTAGE ˚   Page: 1 ˚ D ˚ E ˚
áá

Episode 9/ 1 tells us that it is Scene 1 of Episode 9.

˚Loc: EXT. tells us that the location for the scene is outdoors.

BYRNES YARD/COTTAGE tells us that the setting is the Byrnes' yard.

˚Page: 1 ˚ D ˚ E ˚ is essentially repeating this information. D and E stand for Day and Exterior respectively.

The use of ááááááááááááááá in the header is a device which is peculiar to *Glenroe* and is a sometime feature of Wesley Burrowes's scripts. Other *Glenroe* contributors might use lines instead.

There is no descriptions of Byrnes' yard or the characters. There's no need; a director or script editor who has been directing *Glenroe* for perhaps two or three years doesn't need to be told what Miley's house looks like.

To *2S Dinny\Teasy means that Dinny and Teasy appear in the same frame – a two-shot.

To 9 Sc. 2 Int. Dinny's Kitchen indicates that the scene that should be beginning on the next page is Episode 9, Scene 2, and is an interior setting in Dinny's kitchen.

The scene selected as the next example is actually, however, Scene 4.

Note: (INT) *means* interrupts *and* MS *means* mid-shot.

From 9 Sc. 3 Int. Morans
sitting room

DAY 1 - LUNCHTIME

/

LUNCHTIME. ABOUT TEN
CUSTOMERS. MICHELLE HANGS UP
UP THE PHONE AND COMES OVER
TO FINBAR, WHO IS BEHIND THE
BAR.

MICHELLE
Finbar do you mind if I go
out?

FINBAR
(SIGHS) You're needed here -

MICHELLE

I know, but you see that was
the childminder. She has to
go home because her mother
cut her foot and it turned
septic, so I have to go and
collect James and leave him
up to me mother -

FINBAR

(INT.) How long'll you be?

MICHELLE

Half an hour.

FINBAR

Go on.

MICHELLE

Thanks

AS SHE IS HEADING FOR THE
DOOR, TEASY COMES OUT OF THE
KITCHEN: PAPERS IN HER HAND,
WEARING GLASSES.

TEASY

(TO MICHELLE) Where are YOU
going?

MICHELLE

Well the childminder rang up
and she has to go home
because her mother has a
septic foot and that means -

TEASY

(INT.) Oh go on -

MICHELLE

Thanks Teasy. Listen did you
ask him?

TEASY

Ask who?

MICHELLE

Dinny. About Spain. You were
going to ask him straight.

TEASY

(SIGHS) Well I didn't... I'm
waitin' for the right moment.
Go on if you're going.

MICHELLE GOES AND TEASY GOES
OVER TO FINBAR, WHO IS PILING
AN ORDER ON A TRAY

How's it going?

FINBAR

(IRRITATED) Well I'm on me
own - can you help me out?

TEASY

I wish I could Finbar, but I
have to go home. I'm a bit
worried about Dinny.

FINBAR

Is he all right?

TEASY

(HESITATES) He's not himself.
(AS RORY COMES IN) maybe
Rory'll give you a hand...

SHE GOES OFF TO THE KITCHEN
AGAIN.
FINBAR GOES TO A TABLE WITH
HIS ORDER.
RORY GOES BEHIND THE BAR AND
RE-EMERGES WITH A CRATE OF
LEMONADE. AS HE COMES OUT
FROM BEHIND THE BAR, HE MEETS
FINBAR COMING BACK, BLOCKING
HIS WAY.

FINBAR

What's that?

RORY

It's a crate of lemonade -
what's it look like?

FINBAR

That's bar stock -

RORY

Yeah and it's heavy... would
you move out of me way.

FINBAR

I'm responsible

RORY

(INT.) Look don't concern
yourself... you only work
here.

RORY BRUSHES PAST HIM AND
GOES. FINBAR WATCHES HIM
ANGRILY.

VOICE

Can we have some service?

To MS Biddy

To 9 Sc. 5 Int. Biddy's
Kitchen

WRITING DOCUMENTARIES

Documentaries are factual accounts of a topic which may utilise many broadcasting techniques such as narration, animation, dramatic reconstruction and so on. While there are no hard and fast rules about documentaries, it is fair to say that most are idea-based and most do not depend on rigid scripting for their structure. Some subjects do lend themselves to scripting more so than others. A historical documentary dealing with reconstructions may be rigidly scripted in advance of a production, with every word in the script being used. You may write an excellent, entertaining script on the subject of your pet passion – exotic butterflies maybe – and find you have to rewrite vast chunks of the script when the person shooting the pictures failed to capture vital footage of display rituals. A screenwriter is in complete control of the script; characters enter and depart at the writer's whim and characters say whatever the writer wants them to. This screenwriter completes a script knowing someone will go out and shoot the corresponding pictures. A documentary-maker seldom has the same security. Your proposed documentary might be on the life cycle of an exotic hairy spider – you might spend three months in the heart of the Amazon basin and fail to find a single one. In this case, the intrepid documentary-maker uses all the footage in a new impromptu documentary on Amazonian jungle-fever and how it affects film crews. Documentaries are therefore commissioned on the basis of an viable proposal as opposed to a smartly bound script.

The first stage in a documentary is the formulation of a *proposal*. This proposal has, as its basis, an idea. You should be able to encapsulate your idea in one line. If you were to make your documentary without a focused idea, then you might end up recording everything you see, hoping a programme will miraculously emerge from your piles of tapes.

Once you know exactly what your documentary subject is, you can be assured that you will know instinctively which areas are irrelevant with little point in developing. A documentary-maker always has far more film than he or she can use; a non-focused idea just adds tape to the piles.

The next stage of the documentary's development is *the approach*. How is the documentary to be constructed? Will animation be used? Will there be voice-overs? If so, by whom? Will the narrator be a comedy actor; a professor, a journalist? Will archival footage be used? Which footage? Will there be dramatic reconstructions? Who will be interviewed? What, bearing in mind items such as budgetary restrictions, will an audience actually see? At all times you should bear in mind the realities of documentary-making.

One of Ireland's leading documentary-makers (whose first documentary, incidentally, was made with a borrowed camera), Alan Gilsenan, has this to say about the formulation of a documentary:

> You need to be able to see it realised, and it's even something I fall into myself when I'm writing things that I like. I go on flights of fancy and it's wonderful and you can see it in your mind's eye but you know that in the reality of a wet Thursday afternoon in October in Fermanagh you're not going to do it. And you have to be very aware that it's a very highly practical medium and for the most part in Ireland the budgets are not going to be exorbitant and therefore you don't have that much leeway, so you need to really see it and understand it in very practical terms. You have to be able to see shots – not shot for shot because obviously that's the director's job – but you do have to have some sense of how it will work practically, and that's very difficult, you know, because in a way that almost goes against a writer from prose or theatre or poetry's natural instinct.

You should bear other facts in mind when putting together a proposal for a funding agency, RTE, or an independent production company.

- The proposal, with a short introduction, should be sent to RTE or a producer you feel is likely to be interested in the concept. Lists of producers are provided in the Independent Producers section. It is worthwhile watching the credits of TV documentaries you admire in order to refine this list.

- A proposal stating the idea and approach for a documentary should not really be more than two or three pages long. If a potential producer is not convinced by the first page, they are unlikely to be persuaded by an additional dozen pages of persuasive argument.

- While documentaries are fully scripted only after the pictures have been recorded, some scripting in advance of a shoot is common; you may write the introduction to your subject in advance, or script a scene which will be performed by actors, reenacting some event. A sample segment, perhaps a few paragraphs from an opening scene, is usually more than adequate in a proposal. You just have to prove that you can write effectively.

- A proposal should contain a paragraph or two about any key features you feel are important. Perhaps you own or have access to some rare footage? Perhaps you have a good relationship with an elusive personality who is your intended subject? Perhaps you have studied the life cycle of the moth for four years in university and hence know it intimately?

- A proposal should have a reasonable budget. Producers have ideas and submissions for far more programmes then they can ever make. When given a choice, a producer is inclined to go for the cheaper option. As a writer you are not expected to know current documentary-making costs. Common sense should tell you whether your idea is viable or not.

So you've written your proposal. What next? The choice is to send it into RTE or to an independent producer for assessment. Alan Gilsenan has this advice:

> I think for a writer the most important stage in the whole process is teaming up with the production company who is going to make the film or the programmes. And I think one of the advantages of watching television is that if you see something you like or if you have a sympathy with or an empathy with, then you might get on those people. There is no point going to a big production company who is perhaps putting forward fifty ideas to RTE or Channel 4 or whoever, who don't have a particular interest in what you are doing and perhaps don't even have an empathy in terms of style or approach or content or even outlook. And you find, and I think this has happened to a lot of writers or people with ideas, that they go to a production company who take it on board as one of those 50 proposals and you get excited and you're hoping something's gonna happen and you don't realise that you're just a drop in an ocean of proposals that are being thrown against the wall in the vague hope that one of them will stick!

It should be said that should the proposed documentary revolve around a controversial political or social event, both sides of the argument should be stated, and it is imperative that an unbiased approach be maintained. If you (the documentary-maker) have some interest in the event (other than an interest to document it), then that should be made clear. A viewer is entitled to know if the documentary on nuclear power is being made by a fully paid-up member of Greenpeace or by British Nuclear Fuels PLC. Failure to announce such pertinent details leaves the documentary-maker open to charges of bias and accusations of making propaganda.

WRITING COMEDY

RTE is not noted for its television comedy. Comedy seems restricted to short skits, sketches, or stand-up routines which are included in a television programme. There are no entire programmes devoted to comedy, and whenever RTE broadcasts a new sitcom, it is inevitably greeted with critical derision. This probably reflects the fact that comedy is perhaps the most difficult of the art forms. Despite notable failures, RTE is committed to developing comedy writing and has instigated a series of sitcom-writing workshops. This is perhaps a response to the perception that a major reason for the failure of comic programmes is that the writing often left much to be desired. There is a shortage of good comedy writers in this country; writers who can write good television-comedy are rarer still. While two sitcoms are being developed from these sitcom workshops, this does not mean that RTE will not welcome new ideas. Short sketches and ideas for sitcoms should be sent to the script editor, Entertainment, Television. In the first instance, do not send complete scripts (unless it is a short sketch for a specific show). The script-editor prefers to see concise outlines listing characters. For more details see RTE Entertainment, page 199.

Comedy is all about the ability to make people laugh, and frankly, you can either write comedy or you can't. Many fine writers can trot out laudable novels or dramas but their comic output is laughable for all the wrong reasons. What can look like an unmissable hit at script stage somehow loses its appeal on its way to the screen. What can leave the TV director crying tears of laughter may leave an audience wondering what the fuss is all about and the critics querying why the programme was made in the first place.

Comedy writing is a serious business and should not be attempted by the sensitive, for comedy is difficult to get right and so very easy to get wrong.

While it is impossible to write comedy using a formula (though some try), it is possible to make some assumptions about the nature of comedy and about what we find funny and why. Knowing what is funny is the first step to recreating it. Some comedy truisms (and there are more) might be these.

- Comedy is offensive. If you are not annoying someone then you've got it wrong. If you write a comedy sketch about someone on the dole you will inevitably get someone complaining that your sketch lampooned the serious topic of unemployment and that being unemployed is not funny.

- Comedy loves the misanthrope. Humour may be found whenever characters are placed in situations they find uncomfortable and encounter people they don't like. A hotelier who doesn't like guests all that much could form the basis of a comedy. A character who distrusts everyone is more appealing than someone who loves everyone. No one really likes nice guys.

- Comedy characters aspire to be elsewhere but always fail. A rag-and-bone man may hope for a middle-class life but never succeeds; a soldier may try to get away from the front but always ends up in the thick of it.

- Comedy loves banana skins. We like to see people fail, we like the idea of horrible things happening to tax inspectors, traffic wardens, mothers-in-law. We do not like the reality. A pompous man falling over is funny; discovering he is blind is deeply distressing. One of the running gags in the hit comedy film *A Fish Called Wanda* was that an old lady's Yorkshire terriers were being killed one by one. One scene where a dog is flattened was reshot. The original scene featured a dog surrounded by blood and gore. The new version had an almost cartoon-like flattened pooch.

- Comedy can to be found in normality. Comic writers point out the pointlessness of everyday objects, of lifestyles, of people's inadequacies.

THE SITCOM

The sitcom or situation comedy evolved from a desire to create an inexpensive television-comedy show. While the subject matter of sitcoms may vary, they have far more in common with each other than you might think. A British, American and even Irish sitcom (when they are made) possess some universal qualities.

- Sitcoms are written so that they can be filmed quickly and economically. There is usually a fixed number of sets. In *Cheers* the main set is the bar, supplemented by Sam's office and the pool-room. The use of a few sets in a controllable environment (indoors, on a sound stage) means that several shows can be quickly recorded one after the other. The fewer sets and negligible location shots mean reduced production expenses.

- Sitcom writers keep their characters on the set. In the series *The Odd Couple*, Oscar will not go out bowling; he's more inclined to stay in on the central set – his and Felix's apartment – playing poker. In *Family Ties*, Alex wouldn't usually go over to his friend's house; he'd wait for them to visit him.

- Sitcoms tend to be of series length (six to eight 30-minute episodes). TV producers favour series. A series builds up an audience. A one-off might not be seen by its intended audience. Economies of scale also mean that a six-part series is far less than six times the cost of a one-off programme.

- A good sitcom is one which has varied, interesting characters who react predictably. In comedy, there is little character development. We just know that Basil is going to react in a cowardly fashion when he sees his wife Sybil striding towards him. For Basil to react in any other way is unthinkable. Blackadder may seem to be softening towards Baldric at the end of an episode, but we know that the very next week, he'll be as nasty as ever.

You should write a sitcom which lends itself to humour. A set should be flexible – it's got to be able to sustain enough action to last for at least six episodes. It is no coincidence that a staple component of most sitcoms is the sitting room combined with a kitchen. People can play cards or eat at a table. A sofa can be used for sitting on or made into an impromptu bed.

A good sitcom is less about gags than about story. Basil beating his stalled car with a branch in frustration is funny; Basil standing up telling a joke well would be out of character.

A sitcom often has its comic premise the so-called 'central contradiction'. This is often where a main character or set of characters is placed in an inappropriate setting. Niall Mathews, head of RTE Television Entertainment, refers to:

> someone as disorganised and as obnoxious as Basil Fawlty looking after a hotel, or *Dad's Army*, where the last line of defence against the horde of German invaders is this mob of misfits, old fellas, they can't even get on with each other, and yet these are the people that are left to defend England, should all else fail.

Sitcoms often have a 'family format'; these contain a far more subtle version of this central contradiction. Families in our society are supposed to get on, be loving, supportive of one another – in sitcoms (as in reality), they don't. These families don't necessary require a blood kinship – *Cheers* to all intents and purposes has a family structure, as does *M*A*S*H*. The comedy is derived from all the inner tensions that develop when a group of people who know each other well are forced to share the same environment. *Roseanne, Nightingales, Bread, Married with Children* and *Family Ties* could be said to fall within this category.

Niall Mathews says that the greatest fault with the sitcom and drama submissions he receives is that they are often:

> non-televisual, the characters are weak, or the story is weak. And to get something that includes all those three, and puts them together cohesively, coherently, originally, and interestingly, is very difficult. Some include one of those, but to get one that puts them all together is very, very rare.

It should also be mentioned that what leaves one person in stitches may leave another cold. Comedy writing is often done in conjunction with a writing partner. This partner improves the comic potential of scenes and can point out the areas where the comedy flags. Writing partners can improve a scene so that they both find it funny. John Cleese and Connie Booth wrote *Fawlty Towers* together. Teams of five or more regularly write the better US comedies.

THE SKETCH

The sketch or brief comic scene had its distant origins in theatre. Short, compact, comic scenes whose simple object was to make people laugh were of immediate attraction to television producers. Short sketches could be parachuted in to a programme ensuring it didn't underrun. While many British and American comedy shows are comprised entirely of sketches, this phenomenon hasn't happened here, yet. The emergence of a vibrant comedy circuit (and performers) will ensure that there is pressure to have such a series in the RTE schedules. The reason why there isn't one at present has probably to do with a paucity of good material which would stretch to a season and the expense of making a sketch-based show. A 30-second gag on location could take a cast and crew an entire day to make. Sketch-writers should in the meantime examine current programming for likely shows which will take material. Material should be sent to the producer of the programme.

W R I T I N G
A N I M A T I O N

Animation refers to a process whereby inanimate objects such as drawings or models are given the illusion of movement when successive positional photographs are run together.

Animation is a slow, laborious business. Each second of screen time requires 24 different photographs. No wonder full-length features take hundreds of artists, years to make. It is no surprise also that animation is expensive; an animated film can cost around £8,000-£10,000 per minute.

While the first films that spring to mind when animation is mentioned are *Tom and Jerry* or perhaps *Snow White,* children's cartoons do not represent the whole industry. Animation is increasingly being used for special effects in feature films: examples include the spaceship scale models in *Stars Wars* and the computer-animated dinosaurs in *Jurassic Park.* Animation is also used in short programme links, introductions, or promotional programmes.

While the Irish animation industry is relatively young, there are companies out there who are developing this art form. One of this country's most prolific animators/producers, Jimmy Murakami, paints a somewhat gloomy picture for the would-be animation writer:

> I have a lot of scripts submitted to me; in fact I have two or three on my desk now. It is true to say that because of the nature of this industry, it is very hard to sell something that is originally produced. It really comes down to something that is well known, you know, I mean a classic idea, something that has already been published – unless of course it's really incredibly good. Even then it has to undergo many stages of development.

It is certainly true that stories which have appeared previously in a different format, such as a novel or a folk tale, are seized on more readily by many animation companies. Established stories do tend to attract production finance – perhaps it's because the TV companies are already familiar with the stories and can easily envision an appropriate slot.

THE MARKET

A factor in the TV companies' decision, it has to be said, is that established stories lend themselves to resale. Some fairy-tales are known internationally, and animators perceive that the animated version could be sold in many different countries. These sales could then finance further animation projects.

It should also be pointed out that an animator has to be practical. It may take upwards of a year to complete an animated film, and animators will need a considerable fee to be reimbursed for this work and therefore aim for international sales if their domestic market pays poorly. Fortunately, animation also happens to be relatively easy to dub into different languages. Bearing their audience in mind, many animation projects feature characters undertaking journeys across several frontiers or are based on actual historical events or characters. Many broadcasters are attracted to programmes which contain some reference to their own country.

Animation projects may seek development funding from the European Media programme (see CARTOON, p.188). The Irish Film Board, recognising the importance of animation, is seeking ways to encourage the art form. It is hoped that it will assist projects by topping up programme development funds. The recent development of Anamú, an animation production company network set up to promote animation, is also encouraging (see Anamú, p. 193).

WHY ANIMATION?

If you intend to write an animation story, you should first of all ask yourself: why choose animation instead of live action?

Animation lends itself to stories which have a highly imaginary content: talking animals, fantasy worlds and weird monsters are common animation components. The non-realistic nature of animation lends itself to work which would be considered too violent for a live-action equivalent. Most children's cartoons contain an extraordinary amount of violence.

Writers/producers also find that animation is an excellent medium for portraying more adult themes. Nudity, sex and sexual politics are increasingly becoming themes of animated programming. The medium lends itself to the portrayal of naked bodies and sexual activities which might be considered too titillating if live performers were used.

WRITING HINTS

When preparing your script, bear in mind the laborious nature of animation. What can take moments to write will take months to produce.

> You can write a green-skinned character who has five spots. The animator will, after a month or so of drawing repeated spots, wish you'd only written one spot; after another month they'll think, why couldn't the creature just be green?
>
> *Steve Woods, animator*

Animation writers should think their scripts through pictorially, and should dispense with everything not vital to the story.

Animation scripts are laid out like film scripts.

WRITING ADVERTISING

Advertisements are screened by RTE, but are mainly produced by independent advertising companies. It is the case that more money, time and research can go into a compact 30-second advertisement than went into the programme it's interrupting.

A company who wishes to advertise a product approaches an advertising agency. It is this agency that is responsible for developing the advertisement for radio and/or television, and for booking and supervising the production company which shoots the advertisement.

Many advertisements broadcast on RTE by multinational companies are made by foreign advertising agencies – sometimes these advertisements are dubbed with Irish voices.

THE PERSONNEL

On most advertisements there are two key persons: the visualiser, who comes up with the pictures for the advertisement; and the copywriter, who writes the script. The person who comes up with the concept – the idea behind the advertisement – may be one of those two or another member of the agency team. Sometimes the client company will have specific ideas they would like to see developed by the advertising company. Obviously, no visualiser is required for radio advertisements.

The copywriter, employed by the agency, is creative and will have a proven writing skills background. The copywriter will probably have a degree in English or have studied journalism; he or she could well have taken a course in copywriting. Copywriters must be well read and aware of current fashion and social trends. They will probably be aged between 25 and 35.

It is very rare for an unknown outsider to write for the agency – the agency has its own creative writing team, after all. Some outsiders do ring up agencies with ideas, but frequently demand large amounts of money from the agency before the idea is submitted. Such approaches are unlikely to be entertained; agencies do not have budgets to buy in idea. If an outsider does propose a good idea or script to an advertising agency and it is accepted as having merit, the idea will be taken by the agency and developed by its own in-house team. The person who came up with the idea would receive a fee from the agency only if the client company wishes to use the resulting advertisement.

THE PROCESS

Once an advertising company secures a contract, they usually employ a research team/company to analyse the market for the product to be advertised. The researchers will furnish the client company with details of the people who might use the product, what their disposable incomes might be, where they live, how many there are, what their attitudes to the product are, when they use the product, how often, why they use it, why not and so on. The advertising agency will see a copy of this research or, preferably, sit in on the meeting when the researchers brief the client company on its findings.

The agency has a team which will develop an advertisement aimed at the target audience as discovered by the researchers. This creative team will be headed up by the account director. The account director drafts up a concise document which will define what the task or objective of the advertisement should be. This one-page document is then passed on to the copywriter and illustrator for further development.

Sean Young, managing director of Young Advertising, one of the leading Irish advertising agencies, says that the document asks and answers several key questions such as:

What is the brand? The answer is not Kellogg's Cornflakes, it is Kellogg's Cornflakes that delivers A, B, C, D, to its target audience. What does the consumer think and feel about it now? What do we want the consumer to think and feel about the brand? Then we ask ourselves the question: what are the real benefits to the customer? You can't tell them that a building society will give them phenomenal rates of interest if the building society doesn't do it. The whole proposition to the consumer has to be credible. Kellogg's Cornflakes will deliver a very fine breakfast cereal – it won't deliver a gourmet breakfast cereal, it's not supposed to; on the other hand it won't deliver an inferior breakfast cereal, it will deliver a very fine breakfast and that's what it should be. The final part of the document indicates what the tone and the feel of the advertisement should be. Should it be bright and modern? Singing and dancing? Should it be laid-back and slow and very sensual like, say, most perfume advertisements?

AWARDS, BURSARIES
AND COMPETITIONS

Arts Council Bursaries. Irish Film Board Funding.
RTE/Anamú Short Script Award. RTE/BBC Script-
Development Fund. RTE/Film Base Shorts. RTE/Irish
Film Board Short Cuts. RTE Live at 3/Royal Liver
Assurance Creative Writing Awards. European
Sources of Funding.

Awards, bursaries and competitions are generally open to any writer born in and/or resident in Ireland. Some additional restrictions may apply. Only paid-up members of Film Base may enter the RTE/Film Base Shorts competition, for example, or only writers who submit a script as part of a producing team may enter the RTE/Irish Film Board Short Cuts competition. These restrictions are viewed with dismay by some writers and with glee by others – it depends on your point of view. The Royal Liver Assurance/*Live at 3* Creative Writing award takes place once a year, has few restrictions, and attracted 18,000 entries in 1993 (at the time of going to press, a decision on whether there would be a 1996 competition or not had yet to be made). The RTE/Film Base Short competition for short film scripts costs £30 to join or £25 (unwaged), and takes place two to three times a year. Each competition seldom receives more than 90 scripts and two scripts are selected for production.

A range of agencies provide bursaries for Irish writers. These bursaries are normally for modest amounts. The money can be used to contribute towards a writer's living expenses while a manuscript is being written; it may be used to subsidise other script-development expenses such as travel costs, research costs, stationary costs, photocopying costs, et cetera. When the film or television programme is finally made, the bursary may be deducted from the writer's total fee. In this scenario, the writer's initial bursary is akin to a novelist's advance. If the film is not made, the writer is not normally expected to repay the debt.

Award-winning or competition-winning writers usually gain more than financial reward. They vastly improve their chances of having their manuscript produced, and they concurrently improve their chances of gaining access to some of the additional awards mentioned in this chapter. Awards tend to have a snowball effect. The more you have, the more you can get.

There are two types of funding currently available for the Irish (or Irish-resident) writer: the writer's bursary, normally awarded to writers to develop script;s and the script-development funds whereby writers need to enter into partnership with producers. This latter category is becoming the dominant form of bursary – broadcasters and funding agencies do not see themselves in the business of funding projects which are unlikely to be filmed or televised. They prefer instead to opt for the project which has a better than average chance of making it on to the big or small screen. It is in your interests to find producers who are willing to back your manuscript. A writer and producer will be eligible to apply for most of the funds mentioned in this chapter. A writer without a producing partner is excluded from others. Most screenwriters, especially emerging writers, do not know many producers. A directory of independent production companies who would be interested in seeing scripts is therefore included in this book.

ARTS COUNCIL BURSARIES

70 Merrion Square, Dublin 2. Tel: (01) 661 1840, (1850) 392 492 (local call charge from anywhere within the country); fax: (01) 676 1302

The Arts Council gives awards in two categories: Film & Video, and individual writers bursaries. While these awards are not necessarily aimed at screenwriters, there is no reason why they cannot apply. Acceptable applications are those with considerable artistic merit or which are experimental in nature. No purely commercial submissions are likely to receive aid. The closing dates for receipt of completed applications depends on the award/bursary applied for. Applicants should normally be resident in Ireland or be Irish citizens, and should use the appropriate forms available from the Council offices.

FILM & VIDEO

Film & Video Awards are open to production teams, usually including at least a producer and writer. Awards are normally made twice a year. In 1995 the closing dates were 23 June and 10 November.

> Projects in any category of film may be submitted. Outline scenarios, production treatments and estimated budget figures will be sought initially, though applicants may be requested to submit more detailed proposals or to attend for interview at a later stage. Proposals of an experimental nature or with emphasis on the concept of film as a visual art are welcome, in which case a detailed outline of the film's form and style should be included.
>
> *Bursaries, Awards and Scholarships (Arts Council handbook)*

The Film & Video Awards, with a total budget of about £50,000, cannot be the sole source of finance for productions. Awards may be between £3,000 and £7,000. Grants are often used to make one-off short films; they may also top up a project's finances when grants or funds have been received elsewhere.

WRITERS' BURSARIES

Bursaries can be used to cover various expenses such as travel, research costs needed to develop any work of a fictional nature (film and TV writing included). Living expenses incurred while the work is being written are also allowable. Bursaries can range from £300 to £5,000.

A separate 'travel' award is available for writers. The maximum award is £750. Awards are not normally given for courses or projects of more than three months' duration. They are not intended for persons wishing to attend college. Applications are assessed four times a year. The closing dates for 1995 applications were 10 February, 12 May, September and 10 November.

Artflight

Artflight is a scheme whereby creative persons can fly free of charge anywhere on the Aer Lingus network. Applicants must satisfy the Council that there is some artistic benefit to be gained from an award. Applications for Artflight awards should be made at least three weeks before the proposed travel date.

The Macaulay Fellowship

The Macaulay Fellowship was established by W.B. Macaulay in honour of President Seán T. O'Kelly, and is awarded on a rotating basis to the visual arts, music and literature. The award is valued at £3,500. Applicants must be under 30 years of age on 30 June in the year of application (or under 35 in exceptional circumstances) and must have been born in Ireland. In 1996 the fellowship is awarded to literature.

IRISH FILM BOARD FUNDING

The Halls, Quay St, Galway. Tel: (091) 613 98

The Film Board awards funding in three different areas: development loans for feature-length films; production finance for feature-length films; and production finance loans for documentaries. A scriptwriter may apply only for the first category; production companies and/or directors may apply for each.

A scriptwriter, of course, is free to apply to individual production companies who might be interested in pushing your script to the Board. The advantage of an established company is that it will have experience of submitting work and will therefore have a comprehensive knowledge of the formats required by the Board. You may know how to write the script, but they will know how to prepare a production schedule.

If you cannot get a company interested in your work, you may still apply to the Board for consideration. They accept submissions in all categories three times a year, usually in January, May and September. Details of exact dates aren't available at the time of going to print; phone for details.

If your script gets a favourable response and you do receive an award for script development, you may later be asked for production details – i.e., they will want to know how the total budget is to be raised, who is producing the film, what their backgrounds are, and so on. Your job as a writer is to write the script, not to produce it; it is therefore best that you do not try to produce your project yourself unless you have production experience. Get a production company involved. The Film Board might be able to suggest an appropriate company to approach, or you could call up several companies and mention that the Film Board has expressed an interest in your work. This should get a positive response from someone.

DEVELOPMENT LOANS FOR FEATURE-LENGTH FICTION FILMS

This is open to individual producers, directors and writers, or to a combination of the same. The Film Board will commit up to a maximum of £25,000, though realistically they will be likely to commit less, so as to service as many applications as possible. The money is primarily concerned with feature film-length script submissions, though the Board will consider proposals for shorter films. A development loan is geared to supporting one or more of the three key elements of the 'pre-production' phase of a film project.

- A complete finished script.;

- A production schedule.

- A production budget.

You are expected to provide the script. A production company will provide (or may suggest someone who may provide) the schedule and budget. Once these elements are in place, the search for production capital can commence.

When applying to the board for a production-development loan, you should set out in detail what exactly the money will be used for. If it's to be used to develop the present script into a finished screenplay, you need to be specific. Perhaps the money is intended for travel expenses, research costs, a screenwriting course, or to keep you, the writer, in food during the rewrites. The Film Board is unable to pay screenplay writers the going rates. The attitude seems to be that it is best to pay five writers something rather than give a single writer a substantial fee. An important part of many script-development budgets is the fee for a 'script doctor'. Most scripts and script-writers benefit from the advice of an experienced script editor. They generally are expensive, but will help turn that script into a viable, finished screenplay.

Your application to the Film Board (there is no formal entry form) should contain as much of the following information as possible.

- Two copies of a treatment and/or script.

- Two- or three-paragraph synopsis.

- Notes on the visual style and genre of the film.

- Notes or directions for further development of the script.

- Details of key production personnel, including their CVs, addresses, phone numbers, et cetera.

- Evidence of ownership of rights, including, if appropriate, signed agreements. There is little point in going to a tremendous amount of work adapting a novel, say, into a cinematic format without ascertaining first if the film rights are available. Don't bother sending in a novel and saying 'This would make a good film.' If there is no accompanying work you're just throwing away good postage. A good novel could be poorly adapted for the screen; a mediocre book could be adapted into a brilliant, cinematic vision.

- Any other relevant material such as the financial prospects.

- A full disclosure of any financial support available to the applicant for the development of the project.

Of course, you may not feel qualified to submit all this detail. That's where the assistance of experienced film-makers and production companies becomes invaluable. The most important item at this early stage is the submission of a good script. A good film script will gain precedence over an assured commercial success such as *Return of the Killer Zombie Nymphos II*. The Film Board will be more encouraging towards creative submissions as opposed to the purely commercial.

PRODUCTION FINANCE LOANS FOR FEATURE-LENGTH FICTION FILMS

This category is open to producers/directors and/or companies. Finance of up to 10 per cent of the total estimated budget of the proposed film is available, and is refundable, generally on the first day of principal photography. Current closing dates, (unavailable at the time of going to press) for the receipt of applications may be obtained by ringing the Board. The Board usually accepts submissions three to four times a year.

Your application for production finance loans should contain a certain amount of information (there is no formal application form).

- Two copies of the film script, not permanently bound.

- A two- or three-paragraph synopsis of the script.

- A breakdown of the principal characters.

- Notes on the visual style of the film.

- Notes on directions for further development of the script, if pertinent.

- Details of key personnel involved in the project, including contact names, addresses, and CVs.

- Details of the budget, including top sheet and cash flow.

- Statement of funding required from the board and projected repayment terms.

- Financing plan, projected income, marketing and distribution strategy.

- Accounts of other financing including terms of repayments;

- Evidence of agreements with any other production companies.

PRODUCTION FINANCE FOR DOCUMENTARIES

A small number of production loans are available to documentary makers. The emphasis is on feature-length documentaries which have some potential for theatrical or festival screening. Producers, directors and companies may apply. The Board is unlikely to facilitate projects where existing funding may come from other sources such as RTE. A maximum of £6,000 may be made available to facilitate the making of the production; this is generally repayable on the first day of principal photography.

There is no particular closing date, and projects are judged on a first-come, first-served basis, and on the amount of budget available to the Board.

There is no formal application form but applications should contain a number of items.

- Two copies of a detailed outline of the proposed film.

- A two- or three-paragraph synopsis.

- Notes on visual style and genre of the documentary.

- Notes on directions for further development of the outline if pertinent.

- Details of key personnel, including contact names, addresses, and CVs.

- Detailed budget including top sheet and cash flow.

- Statement of funding required from the board, and schedule of repayment.

- Financing plan, projected income, marketing and distribution strategy.

- Evidence of financial agreements with other production companies, together with terms of repayment.

RTE/ANAMÚ SHORT SCRIPT AWARDS

Arthouse, 5 Aston Quay, Temple Bar, Dublin 2. Tel: No details available

In 1994, Anamú and RTE established a new animation awards scheme. Although it is hoped that the awards will continue, there are no concrete details available at the time of going to press. For more information contact Anamú. Proposals for the first awards needed to include a script, materials required, a schedule and some idea of artwork. The criteria for eligibility were:

*   any style of animation was acceptable which could be rendered by a frame-by-frame process;

*   projects should be of between two and ten minutes' duration;

*   applicants should have some experience of animation production.

RTE/BBC SCRIPT-DEVELOPMENT FUND

David Blake-Knox, Assistant Director of Television Programmes, RTE, Donnybrook, Dublin 4

This, as the name suggests, is a script-development fund for writers set up by RTE, BBC, NI and BBC London, who meet quarterly to assess submissions. The project was set up in August 1992. Up to £50,000 per year is available, and is aimed at supporting a TV writers or contributing towards their expenses while they develop their screenplays. Legitimate expenses might include living expenses, travel or research costs.

As this is a script-development fund, there is no point in submitting final drafts of TV scripts which do not need development.

Successful applications require the support of both RTE, BBC NI and BBC London.

David Blake Knox, Assistant Director of Television Programmes, says that the purpose of the fund is to:

> provide for the development of drama proposals which are based on treatments, or works of fiction, or works of non-fiction, or screenplays or play scripts. But in all cases it should be remembered that this is a script-development fund – not a production fund. For that reason there is little point in submitting final drafts of scripts – since these may not require much further development. The proposals may deal with any subject, and be of any duration or form – provided they are deemed to have a particular relevance to Ireland and an Irish audience.

There is no specific application form required for this fund. Applicants should send in a brief covering letter, a treatment of the proposed script, sample scenes (if any), character and visual style notes.

Some samples of scripts which have been supported by this fund are: *The Last Ditch* (an adaptation of a Roy Bradford novel) by Graham Reid; *Joanne* by Tom McGurk, which is based on the Kerry Babies story; *Ballykissangel*, a six-part popular drama series by Kieran Prendiville; and *The Signal Box* by Barry Devlin.

At the time of going to press, *Ballykissangel* has been completed by BBC NI, and *The Signal Box* has been produced by RTE and scheduled to be screened in the autumn of 1995.

R T E / F I L M   B A S E
S H O R T S

C/o Irish Film Centre, 6 Eustace St, Dublin 1. Tel: (01) 679 6716; fax: 679 6717

This a short film competition organised about three times a year in conjunction with RTE and Film Base. Two films from each session are normally selected for production support. Film Base and RTE assist in the making of the winning films. Successful applicants will receive about £2,500 – £5,000 worth of assistance. Any financial assistance does not usually include writer's fees. A typical feature of the 'Shorts' is that everyone works for free. The completed winning film, if up to the required standard, is normally offered the opportunity of being transmitted on the RTE broadcasting network, during perhaps the 'Debut' season (a season of short films shown on RTE during the Autumn or Spring schedules). Closing dates for receipt of submissions are announced in *Film Ireland*. The criteria for eligibility are:

• films should normally be between five and fifteen minutes' duration;

• films must be capable of being produced within the budget;

• the competition is open to anyone who is a paid-up member of Film Base.

Proposals should include:

• a complete script;

• a list of key people involved in the submission (if any);

• notes indicating how the production can be made using the available funds. You should mention any additional sources of available finance, if known, and/or any equipment/premises needed for the shoot to which you have free access.

If you're writing a low-budget film, you should bear certain factors in mind.

- Avoid historical dramas – period costumes and fixtures are expensive when hired/made in any number.

- Avoid crowd scenes – you may have a small army of friends who will consent to be in your movie without being paid, but they may expect sustenance/travel expenses.

- Avoid special effects as they are often highly expensive.

- Avoid set building. Use existing structures instead. Try to make multiple uses of the same set. Perhaps one draft of your script has the characters eating in a coffee shop and drinking in a pub – maybe both scenes could be rewritten to take place in just the pub.

- Avoid scripts which requires each scene be shot in a different part of the country. Travel and accommodation expenses can multiply at an alarming rate.

- Avoid scripts which are obviously pruned-back versions of feature films. A short film can tell only a limited number of stories. If it tries to address too many issues, it may address none well.

- Use your contacts. If you want to write a story set on a boat, write it with your third cousin's yacht in mind.

- Use characters which can be easily cast. It is notoriously difficult to cast parts requiring very young children or elderly actors.

- Use time well. Try to write scripts that can be shot in a few days. Many actors who are household names have given their time freely to low-budget film-makers. They are likely to shy away from films requiring lengthy commitments. In the same way, your unpaid crew might not be able to take weeks off from the 'day job' to make your film.

RTE / IRISH FILM BOARD SHORT CUTS

IFB, The Halls, Quay St, Galway. Tel: (091) 61398; fax: (091) 61405 or Independent Productions Unit, RTE Donnybrook, Dublin 4. Tel: (01) 208 3015; fax: (01) 208 2510

Until the reconstitution of Bord Scannán na hÉireann, RTE was considered the next best thing to a film board. It encouraged new writing and had a remit (which became mandatory in 1993) to produce a certain number of home-produced programmes. The Film Board is in the business of making films, some of which will ultimately make it to the small screen. The logical step has been the development of a new joint scheme between RTE and the Film Board. In 1994, 'Short Cuts' was established to 'encourage new talent in all areas of film production'. It was planned that £30,000 would be granted to each of six projects.

This production fund is geared towards the making of short films which may be shown in the cinema and later broadcast by RTE. It is not clear whether there will be a 1996 'Short Cuts,' and if so, what format it will take. At the time of going to press there are no details available of successful applicants. Details for the first submission are given below merely as a guideline for future applicants. Be warned: the entry requirements may change, so it is worthwhile double-checking with the Film Board or RTE.

The original emphasis in script submissions was on:

> new film-makers with imagination, visual flair and a commitment to cinema, who will produce original fiction which takes a fresh look at contemporary Ireland. Special attention will be given to new directors, writers and producers.

The first competition required a completed application form available from the IPU, RTE, or the Film Board. The proposal also required two copies of:

- the script;

- the writer's, director's and producer's CV;

- detailed notes as to the proposed style and form of the project;

- budget summaries;

- one VHS or U-Matic show-reel demonstrating some of the intending director's past work. This could either be a complete film or a simple exercise using a domestic camcorder.

Applicants must be of Irish birth or residence, must label clearly all submitted tapes and submit them at their own risk. Keep the originals.

Applications should not be faxed in.

RTE LIVE AT 3 /
ROYAL LIVER
ASSURANCE
CREATIVE WRITING
AWARDS

PO Box 4365, Dublin 4

This is a new awards scheme for writers, which is the result of a collaboration between the Royal Liver Assurance Company and the RTE daytime show *Live at 3*. The awards are broken down into three categories: a schools' section, a poetry section, and a short story section. Details of the 1996 awards (if any) are not available at the time of going to press.

Details outlined here are based on the last competition.

Winners of the short story and poetry section can expect to receive £2,000 each, and the winner of the schools section receives a prize worth £1,000. The winners plus ten runners-up are published in a special, commemorative book. The writers do not receive reimbursement for this publication, the proceeds of which go to charity.

The closing date for entries is usually in November; your application must be accompanied by an entry form available at Royal Liver offices. The basic entry form requires that you fill in your name, address, contact phone number and the category that you are entering.

There are no age limits in the poetry or short-story competition; anyone can enter and there is at present no entry fee. You may not, however, submit more than four pieces of work. Short stories should be no longer than 1,500 words and poems should not exceed forty lines.

Schools may submit as many entries as they wish, as long as the entries are from different pupils.

In 1994 – the first year of the awards – there were 18,000 entries. The short story competition was won by a Dublin barman, the poetry section by a seventy-year-old woman, and the school prize by a ten-year-old Belfast girl.

A short list of the entries is assembled and presented to noted poet Brendan Kennelly, who selects the winners. In tandem with the competition, Brendan gives a series of talks around the country at which he reads excerpts from previous winner's writings, and answers questions. In October 1994, for example, Brendan gave talks in Dublin, Sligo, Kilkenny, Cork, and Waterford. The venues are usually packed and hence require booking. Details of his itinerary are on the application form.

EUROPEAN SOURCES OF FUNDING

Media Desk, Irish Film Centre, 6 Eustace St, Dublin 2. Tel: (01) 679 5744; Media Antenna Galway. Tel: (091) 672 62

The establishment by the European Community of the so called MEDIA Programme in 1991 has meant increased opportunities for writers and film-makers. It was set up to promote the further development of the European audiovisual industry by encouraging the establishment of cross-border networks, enhancing training opportunities, assisting in the development of production projects, and promoting the distribution of programmes. Its success has led to the formation of MEDIA II, an expanded version of this initial five year programme. It is envisioned that all the original MEDIA features will be incorporated in MEDIA II. Significant changes should include the provision of extra funding. As no MEDIA II information is yet available, the details given here are for MEDIA I. With luck, the figures outlined on these pages will significantly under-represent the MEDIA II provisions.

The MEDIA Programme contains several development schemes for film-makers; those most pertinent to writers and/or writers/producers would be the CARTOON, DOCUMENTARY, the European Script Fund and the SOURCES programmes. MEDIA recognises that it is often a shortage of cash and not talent which stymies the development of film projects. A timely injection of capital during a script's development increases that script's chances of being filmed. The programme does not offer subsidies; it offers seed funding to get projects off the ground. Aid is generally in the form of loans which are repayable on completion of the film/TV project. Loans are in ECUs and are available to anyone in the European Union, as well as the residents of Iceland, Norway, Sweden, Finland, Austria and Hungary. Application forms and further information are available from the MEDIA Desk.

CARTOON

Corinne Jenart, Director, 418 Boulevard Lambermont, B-1030 Brussels. Tel: 32 2 245 12 00

CARTOON is a European initiative whose purpose is the development of the European animation industry. It provides financial and training assistance to professional members of the animation industry.

Applications for assistance are accepted twice a year – normally on 31 March and 31 October. Only scripts which are of at least 50 minutes in duration are considered for development. This pre-production aid can be anything from 5,000 to 35,000 ECUs.

For more information contact the above, or the Media Desk.

DOCUMENTARY

Project Development, John Marshall, Secretary General, 29A Skindergade, DK 1159, Copenhagen K. Tel: 45 33 15 00 99

As the name suggests, this is an incentive programme for documentary-makers. The aim of this initiative is the development of the documentary craft. Project-development loans of up to 15,000 ECU are available, and these must be geared towards the development of a project to a point where it is likely to secure additional funding.

These interest-free loans are repayable when the finalised programme is sold.

Applications may be made three times a year. The scheme is open only to producers within the European Community. In order to access such funding, documentary writers are therefore advised to establish contact with a producer.

EUROPEAN SCRIPT FUND

David Kavanagh, General Manager, 39C Highbury Place, London N5 1QP. Tel: (0171) 226 9903; fax: (0171) 354 2706

The European Script Fund is open to writers and producers within the European Community. It is aimed at the development of film and television fiction. All formats, genres and lengths are considered. The ESF (sometimes referred to as just SCRIPT) lends money to producers and writers for the development of projects. This naturally encompasses script development. Loans are repayable when the film or television programme is ultimately made. The ESF functions rather like a publisher giving an 'advance' to its authors. These advances seldom exceed 37,500 ECU. A writer's loan does not normally exceed 5,000 ECU.

The ESF favours stories of interest to several countries. Stories likely to need a co-development partner in a country other than the one from which the submission is received are preferred. Hint: avoid dramas about 1950s Ireland or *Romeo and Juliet*-type stories where one character is a Northern Protestant/soldier and the other a Catholic/terrorist – they've quite enough.

The ESF has funded a variety of projects such as a Spanish sitcom, a French opera, an experimental Dutch TV series and an Italian costume drama. Previous Irish recipients of awards have included Peter Sheridan, for *Kathleen,* a film about about an elderly, feisty woman who becomes a surrogate mother to an orphaned young man; Johnny Gogan for *The Last Bus Home,* about a couple who remember what it was like living in Dublin, ten years earlier; Gabriel Byrne for *The Last of the High Kings,* about a seventeen-year-old during his first summer after leaving school; Barry Devlin for *All Things Bright and Beautiful,* about a ten-year-old who sees a vision of the Virgin Mary and becomes a temporary saint; Jennifer Johnston for *Fool's Sanctuary,* about childhood loyalties tested by the Troubles.

APPLYING TO EUROPE

Application forms are available from the ESF or from the MEDIA Desk. Applications are invited twice a year. While writers may submit as individuals, the material required makes partnership with a producer desirable, and with a production company preferable. You, of course, enhance your chances of having a script accepted by a producer or company if you have your material already assembled – it looks better than ringing up a producer and saying that you've an idea for a film.

If you're interested in applying, start preparing as much of the following information as possible, now. Complete the application form. This form requires you to furnish the following information:

- the title of the work, and whether it is an original work or adaptation. If it is an adaptation, the name and author of the original source material are required;

- the name and function of the contact person;

- the company name, if applicable, and its address, phone, and fax number. The country where the company is based;

- the names and nationality of the writer, director and producer;

- proposed format: will the final film be a TV series, a feature film, a serial, musical, et cetera? Will it be on 16mm or 35mm film?;

- the proposed development budget (in ECUs), proposed sources of development finance, the estimated production cost, and the proposed sources of production finance;

- estimated costs, if applicable, for research, travel, legal fees, writer's fee, stationery, option fees, preparation of budget plan expenses.

The fund is aimed at developing new scripts for television and submissions are judged on their likelihood of making it into production and the creative merits of the programme itself. Of course, the ESF is not going to hand over an ECU until they've had a peek at your script. They will want you to provide comprehensive information detailing the nuances of your script. When applying to the ESF for funding, you will be asked to provide two copies of the following:

- a brief synopsis of the story, which should include references to the setting, characters, and plot. This synopsis will serve as a preface to the treatment;

- a treatment of approximately twelve pages;

- comments on the style, visual elements, pace and structure, and a brief description of the characters;

- a sample scene with dialogue, of about six pages;

- a statement of the writer's fee for the first draft in ECUs;

- a declaration that the project is the original work of the writer. If it is sourced from elsewhere, proof of your right to adapt the material is required;

- a statement as to whether you have been or propose to be in touch with a potential producer, financier, director or agent. Details of your progress should be enclosed;

- biographies of yourself and any other key creative personnel involved.

While much of the above information does seem daunting, most of it, such as treatments, character breakdowns, et cetera, will be material which you as a writer should be assembling anyway. Material gathered for this application can be recycled by you later on and put into other submissions.

SOURCES (Stimulating OUtstanding Resources for Creative European Screenwriting)

Dick Willemsen, Secretary General, 92 Jan Luykenstraat, NL, 1071 CT Amsterdam. Tel: 31 20 672 0801; fax: 31 20 672 0399

The primary objective of SOURCES, established as part of the MEDIA programme, is to 'create inspiring and stimulating sessions for professional screenwriters and film/television-makers in Europe during the development of their scripts'. This development programme is open to screenwriters who have a particular project which is likely to be produced. The script should be aimed at the European market, and be of interest to a European audience.

The development takes the form of two workshops, each lasting a full week, which take place during the drafting of the script. Each session takes place in a different country and consists of four small groups of six writers. There may be an initial workshop dealing with the draft phase of the script, and another when the script is at an advanced stage. Intervals between workshops allow time for redrafting. Workshops take place four times a year.

While SOURCES will subsidise your accommodation costs for the workshops, you will be expected to pay your own travelling expenses as well as a 'participation fee' of between 500 and 1,500 ECU.

Application forms are available from the Media Desk or SOURCES.

ORGANISATIONS

There is a range of organisations which can assist the aspiring and professional writer. Details such as contact names and addresses, while accurate at the time of going to press, are of course prone to change.

A N A M Ú

Arthouse, 5 Aston Quay, Temple Bar, Dublin 2.

Anamú is a newly formed networking organisation based in Dublin's Temple Bar area. It is comprised of Irish animators from independent and low-budget backgrounds, and employees from the larger studios. The organisation is devoted to the development of the Irish animation industry, and intends to raise the profile of animation in Ireland. It also assists the animator by providing information on potential sources of funding, animation courses and so on. It publishes a booklet, *Anamú Animation Directory*, priced at £1, which contains details of Irish animation companies. It is available from the Anamú offices. Anamú, in conjunction with RTE has initiated an animation competition: see RTE/Anamú Animation Award page 180.

A R T S   C O U N C I L

70 Merrion Square, Dublin 2. Tel: (01) 661 1840, (1850) 392 492 (local call charge from anywhere within the country); fax: (01) 676 1302

The Arts Council/An Chomhairle Ealaíon is responsible for the promotion of the arts in the Irish Republic. It subsidises theatres, sponsors dance companies, doles out awards to writers, artists, et cetera. With such a broad brief and limited budget it cannot be nor does it intend to become the dominant entity in the Irish film/TV industry. It does have a film and video budget, which allocates development funds to individual film-makers and screenwriters. These funds are not substantial. Financial aid, if granted, to film/TV projects normally hovers somewhere between about £4,000 and £10,000 per application. For more details see Arts Council Bursaries, page 173.

B B C   N I

Broadcasting House, Ormeau Ave., Belfast BT2 8HQ. Tel: (01232) 338 000

The British Broadcasting Company operates two television stations as well as several radio channels. BBC NI (Northern Ireland) takes broadcasting responsibility for Northern Ireland. This proximity has led to the development of close links between RTE and the BBC. Some programmes are thus funded jointly by both broadcasters (normally the BBC, with its greater revenues, contributes more). A recent development of particular interest to potential screenwriters is the formation of an RTE/BBC script-development fund, which is geared towards developing new scripts suitable for broadcast on both broadcasting networks. For more details see RTE/BBC Script Development Fund, page 180.

F I L M   B A S E

Irish Film Centre, 6 Eustace St, Dublin 2. Tel: (01) 679 6716; fax: (01) 679 6717

Film Base – partially funded by the Arts Council – is geared towards providing resources and information to assist the promotion of an indigenous film culture in Ireland. Its offices provide film-making equipment at low rental as well as a film information service. In the main it is frequented by low-budget film-makers. It is a useful contact point for persons hoping to break into film by gaining experience working on low-budget films for little or no pay. The notice-board in particular is a useful tool; it contains advertisements by writers looking for work, casting requirements for small films, and so on.

The organisation also runs various courses and seminars which are advertised in its offices and publishes *Film Ireland* every two months. As its eponymous title suggests *Film Ireland* is about film-making in Ireland. The magazine has contained features on screenwriting, low-budget film-making, scriptwriting competitions, scriptwriting awards, as well as reviews and interviews with well-known directors and so on. It is available free with Film Base membership or over the counter in retail outlets.

Film Base membership sometimes provides reduced rates for courses and seminars. Membership lasts for a year and may be taken out any time. At the time of going to press, membership costs £55 (corporate/group rate), £30 (normal rate), £25 (reduced rate).

Film Base, in conjunction with RTE, runs a series of short film competitions open to any writer who is a member of Film Base. They are known as the Film Base/RTE Shorts Awards. For more information see RTE/Film Base Shorts, page 182.

IRISH FILM BOARD

The Halls, Quay St, Galway. Tel: (091) 61398; fax: (091) 61405

The Irish Film Board (Bord Scannán na hÉireann) is funded by Dáil Éireann which will, it is hoped, award it around £3,000,000 a year until at least 1997. The board itself does not produce film. It exists to promote film-making in a number of ways, including the provision of development loans or grants to scriptwriters and/or film production companies. This money is usually repayable on the first day of shooting. If, for whatever reason, the film is not ultimately completed you will not usually be expected to return the money; but, the Board is unlikely to continue to advance money to production teams who consistently fail to produce films. For more details see Irish Film Board Funding, page 175, and RTE/Film Board Short Cuts, page 184.

MEDIA DESK IRELAND

Irish Film Centre, 6 Eustace St, Dublin 2. Tel: (01) 679 5744. Media Antenna Galway. Tel: (091) 672 62

This is a European film information service designed to encourage the development of the audio-visual production industry. It is financed and supported by the European Community, the Irish Film Institute, Film Makers Ireland, Dublin City University, Film Base, Bord Scannán na hÉireann and Radio Telefís Éireann. It is open during office hours and is often the first stop for writers and producers seeking information, contacts or simply entry forms for the various European funding agencies and awards as outlined in European Sources of Funding, p 187.

R T E

Donnybrook, Dublin 4. Tel. (01) 208 3111

Radio Telefís Éireann is the Irish state broadcasting service with statutory responsibility for broadcasting within the Irish Republic. It operates two television channels, RTE 1 and Network 2. There is also an additional proposed station Teilifís na Gaeilge, an Irish-language channel scheduled to begin operation in 1996. (see Teilifís na Gaeilge, page 202). RTE manages several radio channels including an Irish-language channel, a popular-music channel, a classical-music FM channel and a talk-radio channel. It also has a symphony orchestra, a chamber orchestra and choir. Its income is derived from a combination of television licences and advertising. RTE's television output consists of a mixture of home-produced programming combined with mainly US and UK bought-in material. Most of its drama budget goes towards its two in-house serials: *Glenroe,* – a rural-based series and *Fair City* – an urban-based series. RTE also co-produces drama with the BBC and other, usually European, television stations. Such co-productions usually require an Irish element or relevance to the proposed drama.

RTE also provides opportunities for writers through the establishment of joint initiatives with other organisations. These initiatives take the form of competitions or awards. The winners are assisted in the development of their ideas and should the end result be up to the required standard, gain access to the RTE network. For further information see:

RTE/Anamú Short Script Award, page 180

RTE/BBC Script Development Fund, page 180

RTE/Film Base Shorts, page 182

RTE/Irish Film Board Short Cuts, page 184

If you have ideas for items – such as sketches – which are intended for inclusion in an existing programme, then you should normally send them to the programme's producer for consideration. Names of producers are listed in *The RTE Guide*.

Ideas for programmes should be sent to the head of the relevant department. The head of a section (they are seldom referred to as departments) will not normally read your proposal. It is usually passed onto a script editor or script associate for assessment. The head will be handed the results of the assessment and will make a decision based on that.

Ideas for features should be sent to: Head of Features TV, RTE. This section is responsible for such programmes as *Head To Toe* and a newly planned arts programme called *Black Box*.

Ideas for youth-oriented programming should be sent to: Head of Young People's Programmes.

Ideas for quiz shows, dramas (other than soaps) should be sent to: Head of Entertainment TV.

There is understandably some overlapping of responsibility. Should a head of department feell that the submission proposal is unsuitable for their section, he or she will pass it onto someone relevant.

RTE is now required by the 1993 Broadcasting Act to use a minimum of 20 per cent of its expenditure on independently produced programming – see Independent Production's Unit, page 201. An independently produced programme will have its production company listed in *The RTE Guide* under the programme's 'tag'. Ideas for that programme or for that production company should be sent directly to that production company. The address may be listed in the back of this book and/or the Yellow Pages. RTE information may also provide you with a contact address.

ENTERTAINMENT TELEVISION

RTE, Donnybrook, Dublin 4. Tel. (01) 208 3111

Entertainment is responsible for a substantial range of RTE's output. Its programming brief includes all in-house drama (with the exception of the soaps), comedy, variety shows, quiz programmes and so on.

The head of the department is known as the managing editor, Entertainment Television. The current editor is Niall Mathews who is responsible for the managing and the commissioning of new in-house programming.

Ideas for comedies, dramas, quiz shows, et cetera, should be sent to the Managing Editor, Entertainment TV.

Vanessa Finlow, drama development editor, offers some illustrative advice on the the needs of television programming. Much of what she says would also be pertinent to anyone submitting non-drama ideas:

> I am interested in developing new talent and new writing, and that is primarily where I see my role in the future. A series like *Two Lives,* which was commissioned from well-known established writers, was one thing we did. What we do have to recognise is that there isn't a culture of television writing in this country and so new writers need to address the needs of the broadcaster. Our needs at the moment fall into two distinct areas. One is comedy and the other is probably something like a thriller/detective series. These are both areas that are specific to the schedule's needs rather than just coming from writers sending in a story idea or a script that may not relate to the

schedule. I think that it is an important factor for new writers to recognise that they are much more likely to raise and generate interest with a series idea rather than a one-off.

What I like to see in a proposal of any kind – I avoid saying specifically 'script' because sometimes the script is actually the last thing I want to see – is something that gives an overview of an idea. In that overview or whatever you want to call it, I want to see that there is a recognition by the writer of the needs of television, crucially that it would in some way meet the needs of this organisation. Having said that, the proposal should also have a strong dramatic idea with essential elements; a well constructed story, appealing characters and an attractive setting.

A multi-million-pound epic about the Famine, say, told in six hour-long episodes, would be most unlikely to ever get very far without substantial co-production input. So it is really unwise for an unknown writer to put a lot of effort into writing six hour-long historical, epic scripts. People should be realistic about the business of television and the business of film. If you want to be a professional writer for the medium, you have to know the business, you have to know who's who, who works where. You have to make it your business to find out what's happening in television. you send something that's badly presented, you put some obstacles in your own way.

INDEPENDENT PRODUCTION UNIT

IPU, RTE, Donnybrook, Dublin 4. Tel: (01) 208 3429; fax: (01) 208 510

RTE has always supported independent producers, either by tendering some programmes to outside companies or by entering into joint production agreements with outside producers. The introduction of the 1993 Broadcasting Act has formalised this relationship. In essence the Act obliges RTE spend a certain percentage of its revenues on the commissioning of programming from the independent sector. The Act states that £12.5 million or 20 per cent of television programme expenditure (whichever is greater) must be allocated to the commissioning of independent television productions by 1999. A further requirement of the Act was the provision of a separate accounting procedure so that the amount of programmes commissioned could be readily ascertained. This has led directly to the formation of the IPU – the Independent Productions Unit – whose sole responsibility is the commissioning and support of independent programming.

The IPU in consultation with the various programme editors, works out in detail the various slots and programme types required in the forthcoming schedules which can be farmed out to the independent sector. Programmes which are not intended to be made in-house are placed out to tender about three times a year. Announcements are made in *The RTE Guide* and national newspapers. Any independent production company is eligible to apply for consideration. Writers, therefore, if they have an idea which they believe is suitable for RTE television, must find a producing partner.

Application forms for commissions are available, from the IPU offices on request. These forms ask for details of contact names/addresses and previous production experience.

In addition to the completed application form, a submission should, where relevant, normally contain:

- a synopsis of the programme's content;

- a treatment;

- the duration in minutes of the proposed programme;

- the number of programmes in the series;

- details of proposed transmission slot and outline of target audience;

- a list of key personnel including producer, director, lighting-cameraperson, editor, cast, writer and presenter, plus their biographies;

- a budget outline, together with a production plan;

- any possible additional sources of funding.

TELIFÍS na GAEILGE

4 Cearnóg Oirear Gael, Domhnach Broc, Baile Áthe Cliath 4, Éire. Teil: (01) 667 0944; fax: (01) 667 0946. Note – the above address is correct at the time of going to press. A new headquarters in the Baile na hAbhann/An Tulach area of the Connemara Gaeltacht is to be built.

Telefís na Gaeilge is a newly proposed Irish station founded with the assistance of RTE. This 'third channel' will ultimately provide two or three hours of Irish- language programmes per day. These programmes are initially to be provided by the independent sector and by RTE. The new channel could also be used for other public-service programming purposes which be cannot adequately catered for on the existing channels – distance education, foreign-language material and Oireachtas material. Teilifís na Gaeilge is at present governed by two separate RTE bodies. The Comhairle is an advisory body set up to advise on the programming and staffing arrangements for TnG. The other body is Seirbhisi Theilifís na Gaeilge which is a wholly owned subsidiary of RTE, manages the business end of the enterprise.

On 25 May 1994, in a series of answers to Parliamentary questions, Arts Minister Michael D. Higgins announced that Teilifís na Gaeilge may not be ready to start broadcasting until 1996.

One of the station's intentions is to stockpile programmes prior to transmission. An advertisement seeking programme proposals was placed in national newspapers in December 1994. While it is too soon to comment on what programmes have been accepted and what writers' markets exist within TnG. It is expected that a wide variety of programmes will be broadcast. Pádhraic Ó Ciardha, Eagarthóir, Forbairt agus Faisnéis (editor, development, media and information) says:

> It is, I think, safe to assume that a third of that output will be children's and young people programming. It is also, given the economics of the thing, fair to assume that about the same proportion of it will be acquisitions which will be re-voiced. We are going to have a news and current affairs output of some kind, and in this day and age you dare not face the public without having a soap. When you put in all those ingredients, I won't say it fills up your schedule, but it gives you a rough idea or a fairly close idea of what we're going to be about.

Writers who have ideas for suitable programmes for the channel but who do not speak Irish should not despair – it is anticipated that much of the material submitted will be in English and will be translated into Irish.

INDEPENDENT PRODUCTION COMPANIES

The companies included in this section were all asked to respond to a set of key questions which were felt to be most commonly asked by writers. While over a hundred Irish companies were approached, only those which are currently interested in producing unsolicited submissions are included. It is worth mentioning that all the companies listed vary considerably – some produce many programmes a year, others produce fewer; some specialise in short films, others are interested only in documentaries. All companies have personnel who submit ideas for development. Unsolicited manuscripts must compete with other unsolicited manuscripts as well as with the in-house project which, all things being equal, will get priority.

Prospective writers increase their chances of getting their work considered if they adopt a professional approach. A good presentation backed up by a good idea will always be seriously considered. Put yourself in the managing director's shoes. Remember, they *want* to make films, it is how they earn their living after all. What is it about your project that will attract them? Does the submission have a clearly defined audience? Where are the likely funding sources? Would the script attract well-known actors? Is the submission tapping into an unknown niche in the market? A good screenwriter knows the ins and outs of production.

Note: Never send original manuscripts. Clear copies only. Include self-addressed envelopes if indicated.

'Writers' refers both to aspiring writers and writers with track records, unless otherwise indicated.

AGTEL COMMUNICATIONS. Production company specialising in corporate, educational and magazine-style broadcasting. It is also interested in producing documentaries and 'broadcast proposals of any nature'. **Founded:** 1980. **Achievements:** six-time winner of ITVA premier award. **Dream submission:** a 'broadcast proposal so good as to guarantee commission.' **Production credits include:** *Ear to the Ground*, a weekly programme broadcast on RTE dealing with rural issues. **In development:** a new, twelve-part food and drink programme. **The approach:** anyone with good ideas may approach in the first instance by phone or post. A SAE is not required for postal submissions. The initial submission should contain a treatment and a project synopsis. **Contact:** *John Cummins, Managing Director, Agtel Communications, Glenageary Office Park, Dun Laoghaire, Co. Dublin.* **Tel:** (01) 285 6833; **fax:** (01) 285 1574. **Response time:** one month.

BANDIT FILMS. Independent production company interested in producing film dramas with 'Dublin' themes and receiving submissions from new writers who possess some film experience. **Founded:** 1990. **Achievements:** winner of Best Irish Short Award at the Galway Film Festival 1990 for *Stephen.* **Dream submission:** a well-written feature film containing an original idea which is contemporary and set in Dublin. **Production credits include:** *Stephen,* a drama; *Bargain Shop,* a TV play about the effects of inner-city development. **In development:** *The Last Bus Home,* a low-budget feature. **The approach:** writers should approach in the first instance by post. A SAE is not required. The initial submission should contain a treatment, a project synopsis and a personal biography. **Contact:** *Paul Donovan, Producer, Bandit Films, Dominick Court, 40-41 Lr Dominick St, Dublin 1.* **Tel:** (01) 873 3199; **fax:** (01) 873 3612. **Response time:** within one month.

BANTER PRODUCTIONS. TV and corporate production company, also interested in producing children's documentaries, wildlife documentaries and children's broadcast and non-broadcast video programming. **Founded:**

1991. **Turn-offs:** 'copycat' submissions. **Production credits include:** *Between the River and the Road,* documentary on inner-city Belfast; *Flight of Fancy,* documentary on pigeon fanciers in NI. **In development:** *3lb 2oz,* short film on sex education and murder; *Friends in Need,* a documentary on German children brought to Ireland in 1946. **The approach:** aspiring writers and anyone with good ideas may contact by phone or post. A SAE is not required. Submissions should include: a treatment, project synopsis, and a personal biography. **Contact:** *Simon Wood, Producer/Director, Banter Productions, 4 Lr Donegal St Place, Belfast, NI.* **Tel:** (01232) 245 495; **fax:** (01232) 326 608. **Response time:** within one month.

BESOM PRODUCTIONS. Film and television production company specialising in feature drama, documentary and education programmes also interested in producing further short, and feature-length dramas. **Founded:** 1991. **Achievements:** the company director was the director of the film *Hush-A-Bye-Baby* which won best drama prize at the 1990 Celtic Film Festival and the 1991 Orleans Film Festival. **Turn-offs:** 'sentimental Irish roots type' dramas. **Dream submission:** something 'germane to the Irish political scene on a personal and mainstream level which is both sexy and wittily written'. **Production credits include:** *NYPD Nude,* a C4 broadcast documentary about a New York police woman who posed nude for *Playboy; Songs and Sounds by Leaps and Bounds,* a C4 broadcast five by fifteen-part music series; *Landscapes,* a children's series. **In development:** *How In God's Name Did I End Up Here?,* a post-cease-fire drama feature. **The approach:** writers should approach by post initially. A SAE is appreciated. The initial submission should contain: a complete script or treatment (with sample scenes), personal biographies and character breakdowns. **Contact:** *Margo Harkin, Film Director and Company Manager, Besom Productions Ltd, 23-25 Shipquay St, Derry City, BT48 6DL, NI.* **Tel:** (01504) 370 303; **fax:** (01504) 370 728. **Response time:** two weeks, though if the company is in production, it can take six months.

BOOTLEG FILMS LTD. Independent production company interested in producing corporate videos, feature films and documentaries. **Founded:** 1993. **Achievements:** received certificates of excellence for *Beyond Reach*, a short film and *Poochers*, a documentary at the Cork, Turin, and Chicago film festivals. **Turn-offs:** Receiving film/video graduate CVs. **Production credits include:** *Beyond Reach, Poochers, The Nook*, and the pop video *Gutter Brothers*. **In development:** *Triple Spiral*, a programme on Ireland's lost wisdom tradition; and two feature scripts. **The approach:** anyone with good ideas may approach by either phone or post. A SAE is appreciated. Initial submissions should contain a treatment. **Contact:** *Denis McArdle, Producer/Director, Bootleg Films, 11 Castle Court, Booterstown Ave., Co. Dublin.* **Tel:** (01) 284 6695; **fax:** (01) 676 0178. **Response time:** within two weeks.

BRIAN WADDELL PRODUCTIONS LTD. Independent video and television production company interested in producing corporate videos, game shows, documentaries, lifestyle programmes (cookery, DIY) and children's dramatised magazine programmes. It would like to get involved with any areas where the ideas are strong enough. **Founded:** 1988. **Achievements:** received the Best Entertainment Programme Award at the Celtic Film and Television Festival for *Fleadh Fever*, and the Erma Best Light Entertainment Programme 1995 for *Festival Virgin*. **Turn-offs:** full-length drama scripts. **Dream submission:** a successful 'low budget' Irish/N. Irish comic or not comic soap. **Production credits include:** *Over the Wall*, two series of a children's dramatised magazine programme containing fifteen episodes each; *Gourmet Ireland*, two cookery series containing fifteen programmes; ten various hour-long single documentaries. **In development:** DIY series commissioned for BBC NI; children's drama series. **The approach:** anyone with good ideas should approach by post. A SAE is not required. Submissions should contain a project synopsis and a personal biography. **Contact:** *Brian Waddell, Managing Director, Brian Waddell Productions Ltd, 5-*

7 Shore Rd, Hollywood, Co. Down, BT18 9AX, NI. **Tel:** (01232) 427 646; **fax:** (01232) 427 922. **Response time:** variable.

CATHAL BLACK FILMS LTD. Independent TV/Film development and production company interested in producing short films, feature films, documentaries and comedy. It would like to become involved in international co-productions. **Founded:** 1988. **Turn-offs:** 'thin ideas' arriving on their desks. **Dream submission:** Well-thought-out scripts. **Production credits include:** *Wheels,* a short drama; *Our Boys,* a short drama; *Pigs,* a TV feature; *Korea,* a theatrical feature. **In development:** *Invisible World,* documentary about spiritual healing; *Hitmen,* a black comedy-drama; *Poachers,* an Irish road movie. **The approach:** anyone with good ideas should approach by phone or post in the first instance. A SAE is not required. The initial submission should contain a synopsis and a finished script. **Contact:** *Cathal Black, Cathal Black Films Ltd, 2nd Floor, 37 Wexford St, Dublin 2.* **Tel:** (01) 475 0216; **fax:** (01) 475 0447. **Response time:** within three weeks.

CAMERA PEN LTD. Production company which develops and produces film and documentaries for theatrical release and broadcast. They are also interested in producing short film dramas, comedy and sitcoms. **Founded:** 1992. **Achievements:** the directors have been in receipt of several grant awards from the European Script Funds. **Turn-offs:** poorly developed, badly presented, unoriginal ideas. **Dream submission:** a fully developed idea, well presented and accompanied by supporting material. **Production credits include:** *My Sister's Hero,* a 100-minute feature drama with a budget of £3,000,000; *33 Auburn Avenue,* a 100-minute feature drama with a £1,000,000 budget; a three-part TV drama series; a six-part television sitcom; a half-hour drama short; a documentary. **The approach:** writers, agents and producers should approach by post. A SAE is appreciated. Submissions should contain: completed scripts, character breakdowns and personal biographies. A submission containing a project synopsis accompanied by a sample scene is also acceptable. **Contact:** *Alison Jackson, Head of Development, 10 River Lane, Shanganagh, Shankill, Co. Dublin.* **Tel:** (01) 282 7033; **fax:** (01) 282 7033. **Response time:** within one month.

DAN DEVANE VIDEO PRODUCTIONS. Independent corporate & training videos production company also interested in becoming involved in local documentaries, heritage programmes and multi-media productions. **Founded:** 1990. **Turn-offs:** 'long scripts.' **Dream submission:** one which would make sound commercial and financial sense. **The approach:** Anyone with good ideas may approach the company by post. A SAE is not required. Submissions should contain a project synopsis. **Contact:** *Dan Devane, Manager, Dan Devane Video Productions, Rock St, Tralee, Co. Kerry.* **Tel:** (066) 27100. **Response time:** within one week.

DAVRAL ENTERTAINMENT LTD. Film production company interested in producing action-oriented films. **Founded:** 1993. **Turn-offs:** submissions which make you 'more depressed than when you started'. **Dream submission:** An 'action adventure in the mould of *Indiana Jones* with the possibility of big-name attractions'. **In development:** *Revenge, Lethal Weapon* set in Dublin; *The Constitution,* American-based courtroom drama; *Body Parts,* a sci-fi 'actioner'. **The approach:** writers should approach by post. A SAE is not required. Submissions should contain a treatment or complete script with character breakdowns. **Contact:** *David Ralph, Managing Director, Davral Entertainment Ltd, 39 Berwick Grove, Swords, Co. Dublin.* **Tel:** (01) 840 0040. **Response time:** between three and four weeks.

DE FACTO FILMS. Film production company interested in producing short film dramas, feature films, and documentaries. **Founded:** 1989. **Achievements:** winner of numerous awards. **Dream submission:** a proposal which has 'already one million pounds raised.' **Production credits include:** *Hush A Bye Baby,* feature was produced by the company director; *Dragons*

Teeth, a short film; *A Long Way to Go*, a documentary; *The Bishop's Story*, a feature film*; More than a Sacrifice*, a documentary; *Everybody's Gone*, a short film. **The approach:** anyone with good ideas should approach by post. A SAE is appreciated. Submissions should contain a treatment, a project synopsis and a personal biography. **Contact:** *Tom Collins, Producer, De Facto Films, 30 Chamberlain St, Derry, NI.* **Tel:** (01504) 260 714; **fax:** (01504) 266 757. **Response time:** three weeks.

EMDEE PRODUCTIONS. Independent TV, corporate and commercials production company also interested in producing short film dramas and documentaries. **Founded:** 1985. **Achievements:** received two Jacob's Awards. **Dream submission:** *Prime Suspect.* **Production credits include:** *Waterways*, a 24-part documentary; *Written in Stone*, a four-part series; *From the Horse's Mouth*, a six-part series. **The approach:** writers should make the initial approach by post. A SAE is appreciated. Submissions should contain a complete script or treatment with sample scenes, a project synopsis, and a personal biography. **Contact:** *Larry Masterson, Executive Producer, Emdee Productions, The Stockyard, 20 Upper Sheriff St, Dublin 1.* **Tel:** (01) 874 1044.

FOREFRONT. Independent video production company interested in producing corporate videos and documentaries (particularly entertainment documentaries). **Founded:** 1985. **Turn-offs:** drama submissions. **Dream submission:** 'lifestyle series' or a documentary revolving around sports or entertainment. **Production credits include:** *Why not Millstreet?*, a behind-the-scenes documentary on the Eurovision Song Contest; *Between the Jigs and the Reels*, a documentary on Fleadh Cheoil 1994. **In development:** a documentary about the Fleadh Cheol 1995. **The approach:** writers should approach by post. A SAE is appreciated. Submissions should contain a treatment, a project synopsis and a personal biography. **Contact:** *Tony McCarthy, Director, Unit 10, Enterprise Centre, North Mall, Cork.* **Tel:** (021) 302 129; **fax:** (021) 302 129. **Response time:** immediate.

GAEL MEDIA. Independent production company with special expertise in Irish-language productions. It would like to become involved in documentaries, game shows and TV dramas. **Founded:** 1990. **Production credits include:** *Musicology,* a fifteen-part music-quiz programme for Network 2; *Celtic Warrior,* a six-part series broadcast on Network 2, UTV and S4C; *Teilifís Pobal,* a four-part series for Network 2; *Seo Sin,* a 30-minute co-production for STV and Grampian; *Life after Dec.,* a 30-minute programme for RTE's *Tuesday File.* **In development:** *Now You're Talking,* a 30-part series co-produced with BBC NI and RTE; *Man on the Move,* a three-part Danish, Jordanian and Irish co-produced series. **The approach:** writers, producers, agents and anyone with good ideas should approach by post. A SAE is appreciated. Submissions should contain a treatment, sample scenes, project synopsis, personal biography, biographies of principals involved, character breakdowns, budget breakdowns, story-board. **Contact:** *Christy King, Managing Director, Gael Media, Na Forbacha, Galway.* **Tel:** (091) 592 888; **fax:** (091) 592 891. **Response time:** one month.

GREG WHEELER PRODUCTIONS LTD. Film production company interested in short film dramas and feature films. **Founded:** 1986. **Achievements:** received various Institute of Creative Advertising Design (ICAD) awards. **Dream submission:** 'a good story set in any area.' **The approach:** anyone with good ideas may approach by either phone or post and no SAE is required. Submissions should contain a treatment, a complete script, personal biographies and character breakdowns. **Contact:** *Greg Wheeler, Film Director, Greg Wheeler Productions Ltd, 9 Prince Edward Terrace Lower, Blackrock, Co. Dublin.* **Tel:** (01) 288 9969; **fax:** (01) 288 9911. **Response time:** within days.

HOFNAFLÚS. Independent production company primarily interested in animation, though would like to become involved in documentaries. **Founded:** 1991. **Achievements:** reached the final of the 'Up and Coming' awards. It recently received the Best Animation Award at the Saar-Lor-Lux film and video festival. **Turn-offs:** 'boring' submissions. **Dream submission:** 'Something different, fresh, unspoilt with a little magic.' **The approach:** anyone with good ideas or writers with experience in children's stories may approach by post in the first instance. A SAE is appreciated. The submission should contain a treatment, a sample scene, project synopsis, personal biography, biography of principals involved, character breakdown and a story-board. **Production credits include:** *A Tale of Two Kitchens*, 26 five-minute clay-animation programmes for children; *Leitirfraic*, a documentary on the history and development of a community over five years. **In development:** *Parafernaliens*, thirteen ten-minute clay-animation programmes for children. **Contact:** *Brid Joyce, Producer, Hofnafk̇s, Unit 2, Casla Industrial Estate, Co. Galway.* **Tel:** (091) 72550; **fax:** (091) 72550. **Response time:** varies.

IGLOO PRODUCTIONS. Film script and ideas development company also interested in producing dramas, feature films and documentaries. **Founded:** 1994. **Achievements:** recipient of various Arts Council and Film Board awards. **Production credits include:** *The Flower and the Rabbit*, a 30-minute TV drama. **In development:** *The Setanta Story*, a documentary on a record company; *Five Little Piggies*, feature film; *Miasma*, feature film; *The Pear Bottle*, a drama. **The approach:** anyone with good ideas may approach. A SAE is not required. Submissions should contain a complete script. **Contact:** *Brian Willis, Producer/Director or Kevin J. Hughes, Writer/Director, Igloo Productions, 1 Vergemount Park, Clonskeagh, Dublin 6.* **Tel:** (01) 269 7639; **fax:** (01) 269 7214. **Response time:** one month.

JAY PRODUCTIONS. Short drama and current affairs programme producer interested in producing corporate videos, short film drama and documentaries. **Founded:** 1992. **Turn-offs:** submissions without an audience in mind. **Dream submission:** A submission with a clearly defined destination in terms of slots on RTE, ITV, BBC or C4. **Production credits include:**

History of the O'Neills, a 40-minute documentary on the O'Neills with Cardinal O'Fiaich and others; *Between the Lines*, a programme on dyslexia; *Handyworks*, short dramas with the handicapped; *Penoptes*, a short film. **The approach:** agents and writers should approach by either phone or post. A SAE is not required. Submissions should contain a treatment, a sample scene, a project synopsis, personal biography, biographies of principals involved. **Contact:** *Mr O'Hanlon, Producer/Director, Jay Productions, 21a Windsor Ave., Belfast, BT9 6EE, NI.* **Tel:** (01232) 661 181; **fax:** (01232) 661 181. **Response time:** depends on the length of the submission.

KEY FEATURE PRODUCTIONS. Feature-film production company with a 'vision for universal cinema around the world', also interested in corporate videos, animation, documentaries and pop videos. **Founded:** 1992. **Achievements:** received the W.H. Hart Award at the New England Film & Television Festival. **Turn-offs:** 'the Person' arriving with the submission. **Dream submission:** ten-minute video version of a potential feature film to get a feel for the project. **Production credits include:** *Celtic Grooves*, a feature music documentary for worldwide audiences; *Keeping the Dream Alive*, an eight-part series on enterprise and entrepreneurs; *Women in the 60s*, a six-part series for WGBH Boston. **In development:** *Summer with Martha*, twenty-something road-film in the USA; *Fearless of Bold*, one boy's fight for survival; *Macheral Skies*, a romantic journey through the Emerald Isle. **The approach:** producers and writers should approach by post. A SAE is appreciated. Submissions should contain a treatment, sample scenes, a complete script, character breakdowns, budget breakdowns and a story board. **Contact:** *Mr. M. Clyne, Director/Producer, Key Feature Productions, The Powerhouse, Pigeon Harbour, Dublin 4.* **Tel:** (01) 668 7155; **fax:** (01) 668 7945. **Response time:** between four and six weeks.

LAGAN PICTURES LTD. Broadcast television production company. primarily interested in dramas and documentaries. **Founded:** 1989.

Achievements: the company director was the producer/director of *The Hidden Curriculum* which won the Michigan State University Samuel G. Engel Award for best foreign drama. **Turn-offs:** receiving 'troubled dramas' or 'love across the barricades' stories or anything with men in balaclavas. **Dream submission:** an original idea for a six-part series set in and reflecting the culture of Northern Ireland. **Production credits include:** *A Force Under Fire*, a 90-minute history of the RUC for UTV. **In development:** several documentaries for Channel 4; *Say Nothing*, a feature-length television film based on a true story. **The approach:** writers, agents and anyone with good ideas should make the initial approach by post. A SAE is not necessary. Submissions should contain a treatment, a project synopsis and a personal biography. **Contact:** *Stephen Butcher, Producer/Director, Lagan Pictures Ltd, 7 Rugby Court, Agincourt Ave., Belfast BT7 1PN. NI.* **Tel:** (01232) 326 125; **fax:** (01232) 326 125. **Response time:** no set time.

MEDIAWISE. Independent TV, documentary, series and corporate video production company interested in producing corporate videos, documentaries, pop videos and broadcast series. **Founded:** 1988. **Achievements:** received an award from Aer Lingus for its provision of in-flight entertainment. **Turn-offs:** submissions which have no research done and no focussed ideas. **Dream submission:** a well-researched idea with a realistic budget and proposals as to where possible sponsorship might come from. **Production credits include:** *Distant Drum,* documentary series. **In development:** *Lemass,* a political and personal biography; *Keneally's Ireland,* Thomas Keneally on the Ireland he knows. **The approach:** anyone with good ideas should approach by phone or post. A SAE is not required. Submissions should contain a treatment, project synopsis, personal biography, biography of principals involved, budget breakdown. **Contact:** *Maxine Brady, Mediawise, 7 Lower Fitzwilliam St, Dublin 2.* **Tel:** (01) 676 8477; **fax:** (01) 676 8470. **Response time:** between two and three weeks.

OCEAN FILM PRODUCTIONS. Independent film, TV drama and documentary production company also interested in short dramas and comedy. Documentaries tend to deal with social, cultural, economic and environmental issues. **Founded:** 1989. **Achievements:** received awards from The Creative DOCUMENTARY fund, Copenhagen, The European Script Fund, the International Celtic Film and Television Festival, and the Arts Council of Ireland. **Dream submission:** original, quirky ideas for film displaying good story-telling. **Production credits include:** *Parent Practice*, a six-part series about the experiences of being a parent in the 1990s for RTE; *The Feeling Soul/An tAnam Mothala*, biographical portrait of Nuala Ní Dhomhnaill which was filmed in Ireland and Turkey for RTE; *Twelve Days to Save the World*, an hour-long feature documentary filmed in Rio de Janeiro offering a view from Brazil after the Earth Summit; *Garret Fitzgerald: A Profile*, documentary of former Taoiseach Garret Fitzgerald for RTE and C4; *The Fair of Ballinasloe*, a 30-minute documentary about the survival of Europe's oldest horse fair for Telegael; *Dr Browne Also Spoke*, a documentary portrait of veteran politician and psychiatrist Dr Noel Browne set on a train for RTE; *Requiem for a Civilisation,* a one hour documentary set in the West of Ireland; *St Patrick: The Living Legend*, an hour-long documentary exploring the historical and social forces that have led to worldwide celebration of St Patrick's Day; *Timeout*, ten short inserts for RTE's Religious Department. **In development:** *The Fifth Province*, a feature film. **The approach:** writers should approach in the first instance by post. A SAE is not required. Submissions should contain a treatment, a sample scene, a project synopsis, and biographies of the principals involved. **Contact:** *Catherine Tiernan, Producer, Ocean Film Productions, The Powerhouse, Pigeonhouse Harbour, Dublin 4.* **Tel:** (01) 668 7155; **fax:** (01) 668 7945. **Response time:** three months.

PANCOM LTD. Video, film, audiovisual and multimedia production and facilities company interested in producing corporate videos, short film dramas, documentaries, pop videos and 'Heritage and Visitor Attractions' . **Founded:** 1992. **Achievements:** the directors have 25 years experience in Audiovisuals. **Production credits include:** *Silver Journey,* a documentary on the first Shannon-to-Erne boat rally; *Some Enchanted Evening,* a 30-minute drama dealing with the occult; *Camera Obscura,* a documentary on the photographer Ivan Wolff. **In development:** *Shadows,* a TV drama series on the subject of Irish ghost stories. **The approach:** writers and anyone with good ideas should approach by phone or post. A SAE is not required. Submissions should contain a treatment and a sample scene. **Contact:** *Keith Nolan, Director, Pancom Ltd, 23 Seapoint Ave., Blackrock, Co. Dublin.* **Tel:** (01) 280 8744; **fax:** (01) 280 8679. **Response time:** one month.

PARADOX PICTURES. Film and video production company interested in producing short film dramas, feature films, comedies, documentaries and pop videos. **Founded:** 1992. **Achievements:** the director has received Arts Council Film Project awards, the top prize for drama at the Bulras Film Festival as well as Fuji scholarship awards. **Turn-offs:** submissions which are neither typed nor legible. **Production credits include:** the short dramas *Sunny's Deliverance, The Barber Shop* and *The Big Swinger.* **In development:** several feature films including, *Northern Lights; Constance and Sarah;* and *Roseland* which begins principal photography in autumn of 1995. **The approach:** Anyone with good ideas should approach by post or phone. A SAE is not required. Submissions should include a treatment, a project synopsis and a personal biography. **Contact:** *Liam O'Neill, Director, Paradox Pictures, 6 Belvedere Place, Dublin 1.* **Tel:** (01) 836 6868; **fax:** (01) 836 6868.

PARTING SHOTS LTD. Film production company interested in producing short film dramas, feature films, documentaries. **Founded:** 1993. **Achievements:** received the Youth Award and several commendations from the Celtic Film Festival for its programming. **Dream submission:** short submissions with radical politics a bonus. **Production credits include:** *Our*

Words Jump to Life, Schizophrenic City, Between Ourselves, Unfinished Business, all for C4; *The Happy Garden* for PBS/SBS. **In development:** A feature film plus documentaries. **The approach:** anyone with good ideas should approach by post. A SAE is not required. Submissions should contain a project synopsis and a personal biography. **Contact:** *Ms Hindman, Producer/Director, Parting Shots Ltd, 4 Lower Donegal St Place, Belfast, BT1 2FN, NI.* **Tel:** (01232) 243 495; **fax:** (01232) 326 608. **Response time:** six weeks.

POOLBEG PRODUCTIONS LTD. Independent film and television production company interested in producing short dramas, feature films, documentaries and pop videos. **Founded:** 1983. **Achievements:** received *Sunday Independent* Arts Awards for the Chicago Film Festival. **Turn-offs:** feeble copies of international hits. **Dream submission:** submissions which display imaginative ideas. **Production credits include:** *At the Cinema Palace,* award winning profile of Liam O'Leary; *In Flags or Flitters; Pictures of Dublin,* archive compilation; *Irish Cinema – Ourselves Alone,* part of international documentary series. **The approach:** anyone with good ideas should approach by post. A SAE is not necessary. Submissions should contain a complete script, a treatment, sample scenes, a project synopsis and a personal biography. **Contact:** *Donald Taylor Black, Chairman & Producer/Director, Poolbeg Productions Ltd, 9 Mount St Crescent, Dublin 2.* **Tel:** (01) 676 2521; **fax:** (01) 284 0958. **Response time:** between four and six weeks.

PREMIER VIDEO PRODUCTIONS. TV and corporate video production company also interested in producing series, short dramas and documentaries. **Founded:** 1987. **Achievements:** praised by the *Sunday Business Post* for its versatility. **Turn-offs:** complicated, bulky, hard-to-read submissions. **Dream submission:** A well presented, easy to read submission. **Production credits include:** *Clonmel Be Proud,* urban renewal documentary; *Tipperary South,* tourist promotional video. **In development:** *Euroair,* a promotional video for a career in piloting. **The approach:** anyone with good ideas should approach by post. A SAE is appreciated. Submissions should contain a treatment or complete script, a budget breakdown, a story-board and ideas of financial sources where development money may be obtained. **Contact:** *Brendan Kerins, Producer/director, Premier Video Productions, Dublin Rd, Cahir, Co. Tipperary.* **Tel:** (052) 41353; **fax:** (052) 41353. **Response time:** between one and two weeks.

ROISÍN RUA. Independent production company interested in producing film dramas. **Founded:** 1992. **Achievements:** winner of four awards at European short film festivals. **Dream submission:** a well-written feature film containing an original idea which is contemporary by a first-time feature writer. **Production credits include:** *The Visit,* a 22-minute drama about a prisoner's wife in the North. **In development:** *Blood Sisters,* a period drama. **The approach:** Writers, who should ideally possess some film experience, should approach in the first instance by post. A SAE is not required. The initial submission should contain a treatment, a project synopsis and a personal biography. **Contact:** *Paul Donovan, Producer, Roisín Rua Films, Dominick Court, 40-41 Lr Dominick St, Dublin 1.* **Tel:** (01) 873 3199; **fax:** (01) 873 3612. **Response time:** one month.

SAMSON FILMS. Film production company interested in short film dramas and feature films. **Founded:** 1984. **Achievements:** director David Collins, who is also executive producer with Radius Television, co-founded Strongbow Film and Television Productions which produced the feature film *Eat the Peach* and the Channel 4 series *When Reason Sleeps.* **Production credits include:** *The Disappearance of Finbar,* a co-production for Film Four International with First City Features (UK) and Victoria Films (Sweden); *The Governor,* a seven-part prime-time series with La Plante Productions for the ITV network; *Guiltrip,* a film written and directed by Gerard Stembridge for Temple Films; *Loving,* a drama based on Henry Green's novel and produced with the BBC. **In development:** *Partytown,* the story of two American soldiers who find love with the members of a theatre company in Dublin during the Second World War; *The Land of Spices*, a story set in 1904 revolving around a Superior of a French religious order who is contemplating leaving the nunhood and meets up with a lonely neglected child; *Eclipsed*, the story of a young, unmarried country girl who is sent to have her baby in a 'magdalen' closed convent; *Ruling Passions*, the recreation of the life of Roger Casement, one of the heroes of The 1916 Rising, directed by Thaddeus O'Sullivan. **The approach:** writers may approach by phone or post. A SAE is not required. **Contact:** *David Collins, Managing Director, Samson Films, The Barracks, 76 Irishtown Rd, Dublin 4.* **Tel:** (01) 667 0533; **fax:** (01) 667 0537. **Response time:** variable.

SCANÁIN DOBHARCHÚ. Independent producer of Irish-language programmes interested in producing short film dramas, comedy and documentaries, especially in Irish. **Founded:** 1992. **Production credits include:** *Teilifís Pobail*, three documentaries for RTE; *Beannacht an Fhomhair*, a documentary on a Church of Ireland community in West Donegal. **In development:** two short dramas for television. **The approach:** writers and anyone with good ideas should approach by either phone or post. A SAE is not required. Submissions should contain a treatment, a sample scene, a project synopsis, and character breakdowns. **Contact:** *Máirín Seoighe, Director, Scanáin Dobharchú, Scrath na Corcra, Na Doirí Beaga, Co. Dhún na nGall.* **Tel:** (075) 32185; **fax:** (071) 32189. **Response time:** between two and three weeks.

SCOTHÓGFÍSE TEO. Drama, documentary and young peoples' programme producer, also interested in producing short film dramas and comedy. **Founded:** 1991. **Achievements:** received a script award for short drama. **Turn-offs:** any futuristic-type material or science fiction. **Dream submission:** a feature film or short dramas relevant to modern Ireland. **Production credits include:** *Sin í an Fhírinne*, a 30-minute documentary on

Connemara poet Johnny Chóil Mhaidhe; *Cás Tíuachríoch*; a 30-minute drama based on a short story by Bryan Mac Mahon; *As Seo Amach*, a six-part series for RTE; *Expose, na Tánaithe i Seville*, 30-minute documentary made with Irish Language Theatre Company at Expo 92 in Seville. **In development:** *Psychosis*, a 30-minute drama; a series on archaeology. **The approach:** writers and anyone with good ideas should approach by phone or post. A SAE is not required. Submissions should contain a treatment, a sample scene, and a project synopsis. **Contact:** *Aodh Ó Coileáin, Producer/Director, Scothohfíse Teo, Abha na Dála, An Daingean, Co. Chiarraí.* **Tel:** (066) 52022, 51937, 51606; **fax:** (066) 51937, 51606. **Response time:** two weeks.

SHORWAY VIDEO INTERNATIONAL LTD. Video production and facilities company interested in producing corporate videos and travelogues though will consider anything submitted. **Founded:** 1985. **The approach:** writers should submit material by either post or phone. A SAE is appreciated. Submissions should contain a complete script. **Contact:** *Stephen J. Shorten, Managing Director, Shorway Video Int. Ltd, Ballylinan, Athy, Co. Kildare.* **Tel:** (0507) 25155; **fax:** (0507) 25155. **Response time:** one month.

SIN SIN TEO. Television production company interested in producing corporate videos, game shows, film dramas, documentaries, arts and Irish programmes. **Founded:** 1993. **Turn-offs:** current affairs. **Dream submission:** Six-part young people's drama in Irish. Production credits include: *Gaeilcheoil Tíre Chonamara*, two 30-minute music programmes; *Celtica*, pilot for celtic arts series; *Rúille Búille,* pilot for light entertainment programme. **In development:** *Ó Ruairc*, youth adventure drama. **The approach:** anyone with good ideas may approach by phone or post. A SAE is appreciated. Submissions should include a treatment, sample scene and a personal biography. **Contact:** *Trevor Ó Clocmartaigh, Leiritheoir, Sin Sin Teo, Cill Bhriocain, Rosmuc, Co. na Gaillimhe.* **Tel:** *(091) 574349;* **fax:** (091) 574346. **Response time:** six weeks.

TREASURE FILMS IRELAND LTD. Independent feature film, TV drama and documentary production company. **Founded:** 1991. **Achievements:** received the Best Irish Short award for *A Stone in the Heart* in Cork, while the director of *Ailsa* won the Premier Enskal Media award in San Sebastian. **Production credits include:** *A Stone in the Heart,* a documentary *Road to America; The Long way Home.* **In development:** *Football Against the Enemy, Cowboys and Indians,* based on the novel by Joe O'Connor. **The approach:** writers, producers and anyone with good ideas should approach by post. A SAE is appreciated. Submissions should contain a treatment, sample scenes, project synopsis and a personal biography. **Contact:** *Robert Walpole, Managing Director, Treasure Films Ltd, Shamrock Chambers, 1-2 Eustace St., Dublin 2.* **Tel:** (01) 670 9609; **fax:** (01) 670 9612. **Response time:** between three and four months.

VERMILLION FILMS. Independent production company interested in producing dramas and documentaries, would like to become more involved in TV drama. **Founded:** 1993. **Dream submission:** *'Casablanca II.'* They'd like a good story, well told with strong characters in tough situations. **Production credits include:** *Recruits,* a series on the Gardaí for RTE. **In development:** *Escape from the Anthill,* drama based on the Fethard-on-Sea boycott of 1957. **The approach:** writers should make the initial approach by post. A SAE is appreciated. **Contact:** *Gerry Greg, Producer, Vermillion Films, 12 Abbey St, Howth, Co. Dublin.* **Tel:** (01) 832 2294; **fax:** (01) 832 3517. **Response time:** one month.

VIDEOACTIVE LTD. Independent television production company. The company is also interested in producing game shows and corporate videos. **Founded:** 1984. **Achievements:** received three ITV Merit Awards and one ITVA Craft Award. The company has had over 300 hours of programming transmitted by RTE and UTV. **Turn-offs:** poorly thought-out treatments or ideas. **Dream submission:** a concise, well-researched, well-developed programme submission complete with substantial funding in place. **Production credits include:** seven series of *Sportsworld* and two series of *Weekend Sport,* also a wide range of young people's programming. **In development:** *In the News,* news-based quiz featuring well-known personalities. **The approach:** writers and producers should approach by post. A SAE is not required. Submissions should include a treatment, project synopsis and a personal biography. **Contact:** *Denis Cregan, Sales and Marketing Director, Videoactive Ltd, Eng House, Tubbermore Rd, Dalkey, Co. Dublin.* **Tel:** (01) 285 4555 (4 lines); **fax:** (01) 285 5942. **Response time:** between one and two months.

USEFUL PUBLICATIONS

Anamú – Animation Directory. Slim publication priced at £1, containing details of Irish animators and animation companies, plus useful addresses and contacts. Available from the Anamú offices, Arthouse, 5 Aston Quay, Temple Bar, Dublin 2.

Bursaries, Awards and Scholarships. A free brochure published by the Arts Council containing details of writers' bursaries and awards. Available from The Arts Council, 70 Merrion Square, Dublin 2. Tel: (01) 661 1840, (1850) 392 492 (local call charge from anywhere in the country).

Film Scriptwriting – a Practical Manual. Dwight V. Swain. Published by Focal Press, USA. A comprehensive step-by-step approach to writing film and TV scripts. A useful guide for the writer, though pricey at about £25.

MEDIA – Guide for the Audiovisual Industry. This free publication is aimed at producers, writers, film and television companies who wish to secure assistance from the EC. It is a comprehensive handbook detailing all aspects of the MEDIA Programme, and is published by the European Community. Copies are available from European MEDIA desks, including the Media Desk in the Irish Film Centre, Eustace St, Dublin 2. A less voluminous synopsis is also available at the same locations.

Prize-winning Radio Stories. Published by Mercier Press. Collection of Francis MacManus radio short-story competition winners. Ideal book for competition entrants.

The RTE Guide. Weekly magazine containing details of Irish television and radio programming. It also contains articles on forthcoming competitions such as the P.J. O'Connor Awards.

Writers' & Artists' Yearbook. Published by A & C Black of London. An updated edition of the book is published annually. This is a helpful guide for any writer. While it contains articles on writing, its most useful feature is the comprehensive listings of potential markets for scripts.

The Writer's Handbook. Comprehensive annual publication listing everything from agents to publishers. Interesting sections on what authors think of particular publishers.

Writing for the BBC. Norman Longmate. A very beneficial publication for the television and/or radio writer. It contains all the postal addresses of the BBC offices around Britain and Northern Ireland, as well as articles on markets within the BBC network. It is available from bookshops and BBC regional offices.

INDEX